Sunset

Appetizers

By the Editors of
Sunset Books and
Sunset Magazine

To the Queen of Snacks.
Maybe there are a few
new ideas within. Mom
Love Sylvie + Steve
Xmas 2000

Sunset Publishing Corporation ■ **Menlo Park, California**

Research & Text
Sue Brownlee

Contributing Editor
Fran Feldman

Coordinating Editor
Gregory J. Kaufman

Design
Joe di Chiarro

Photographers
Darrow M. Watt: 38. **Tom Wyatt:** 3, 6, 11, 14, 19, 22, 27, 30, 43, 46, 51, 70, 75, 91. **Nikolay Zurek:** 35, 54, 59, 62, 67, 78, 83, 86, 94.

Photo Stylists
Susan Massey-Weil: 3, 6, 11, 14, 19, 27, 30, 43, 46, 51, 59, 62, 70, 75, 83, 86, 91. **Lynne B. Tremble:** 35, 38, 54, 67. **JoAnn Masaoka Van Atta:** 22, 78, 94.

SUPER STARTERS

Whether you're looking for easy-to-prepare appetizers, simple between-meal snacks, or elegant starters, you'll find a satisfying selection of dips, spreads, and hot and cold tidbits served up in this book.

Especially designed for the busy cook who wants make-ahead convenience along with sophisticated good taste, our recipes offer an appetizing assortment of options featuring eggs and cheese, fresh fruit and vegetables, and meats, poultry, and seafood. Choose from different cuisines, delicious seasonal fare, and even microwave possibilities.

Our party menu suggestions and planning hints provide for relaxed entertaining that can be enjoyed by both the guests and the cook.

Our thanks go to Barbara Szerlip for carefully editing the manuscript and to Joan Erickson for her editorial assistance. We also thank Laurin Lynch for her help with food styling; Susan Jaekel for the illustration on page 1; Fillamento, Cookin', Cottonwood, The Best of All Worlds, and Pic-Nic-Nac for props; and Schaub's Meat, Fish & Poultry, Monterey Market, Village Cheese House, and Draeger's Supermarket, Inc., for their generosity and help.

For our recipes, we provide a nutritional analysis (see page 5) prepared by Hill Nutrition Associates, Inc., of Florida.

About the Recipes

All of the recipes in this book were tested and developed in the *Sunset* test kitchens.

Food and Entertaining Editor
Sunset Magazine
Jerry Anne Di Vecchio

Cover: Black bean dip with jicama chips, recipe on page 15. Design by Jean Warboy; photography by Noel Barnhurst; food styling by George Dolese; art direction by Vasken Guiragossian.

VP, Editorial Director, Sunset Books: Bob Doyle

6 7 8 9 0 QPD/QPD 9 8 7 6 5 4 3 2 1 0

Please visit our website at www.sunsetbooks.com

CONTENTS

Cocktail Cream Puffs (recipe on page 73)

GREAT BEGINNINGS

Appetizers—creamy dips, chunky spreads, hot tidbits, and cold canapés —are delightful appetite enhancers. They can introduce a dinner, serve as between-meal snacks, or provide party sustenance all on their own.

Hors d'oeuvres should be enjoyed by both the guests and the cook. Literally "outside the main work," these additions to a basic menu don't have to overwhelm the cook with extra effort. Understanding what's involved can make even an all-appetizer event a breeze to prepare. The key to success is careful planning.

Variety. Plan to offer a varied assortment of appetizers that invites tasting a bit of everything. Your choices should include both hot and cold foods, keeping in mind, of course, your refrigerator, freezer, and oven space.

It's a good idea to contrast texture as well as temperature in your selections. Offer a balance between crunchy and smooth, delicate and dense. And mix appetizers that need to be passed with those that guests can serve themselves.

Plan on variety in flavors, too. Add spark with spices, but offer mild alternatives for the less adventuresome. Your company will also appreciate rich treats tempered by refreshingly light ones. And don't focus on a single taste; although everyone may enjoy basil, garlic, or lemon, use such flavorings as accents, rather than in every dish.

If you're planning a large appetizers-only party, serve at least one appetizer from each of the following categories: eggs and cheese; breads; meat and poultry; fish and shellfish; and vegetables and fruits. If you're choosing hors d'oeuvres to offer before dinner, try to complement the main course in taste, texture, and temperature.

Keep an eye on your selections so that colors harmonize with each other on your table. The fresh herbs, fruits, and vegetables you choose can brighten and tie together your presentation.

Quantity. For most cooks, the biggest problem is deciding how much food to prepare. Weather and time of day affect your guests' appetites: people tend to eat more in cold weather; appetites are also heartier in the early evening than in mid-afternoon. And be sure to keep in mind the rest of your menu. If you're planning a heavy dinner to follow, a few light appetizers (perhaps one passed, one serve-yourself) should suffice.

For an all-appetizer party, prepare at least two servings or pieces per person of each hors d'oeuvre you plan to pass; offer at least six different types of passed appetizers each

hour. Supplement them with food that guests can serve themselves, such as dips, spreads, and cheeses.

Time. You'll appreciate your event more—and so will your guests—if you're out of the kitchen and part of the party. Do your marketing well in advance and prepare as many dishes as possible ahead of time. Make sure you can easily handle those that require last-minute effort.

When you freeze, use specially designed freezer wraps and containers, and follow the storage guidelines in the recipe. Remember that recipes relying on potatoes, cooked noodles, rice, fried tortillas, and hard-cooked egg whites can change texture when frozen; emulsions, like mayonnaise and hollandaise, and foods in cream sauce are also not very successful freezer candidates.

Easy extras. Budgeting your time frees you for finishing touches. You'll be amazed at how effectively a few simple garnishes can dress up your dishes without taxing your patience or ability.

Cut carrots diagonally and fan them for a pretty floral effect. Run a fork down the sides of an unpeeled cucumber and then slice it crosswise for an attractive pattern. Thinly sliver both ends of green onion sections several times lengthwise and place in ice water until ready to use as flowers. Cut a lemon slice to the center and flip one end for a three-dimen-

sional presentation. Or try a star-topped mushroom: press the tip of a pointed knife five times around the center of each mushroom to form a star.

Beverages. Just as with food, your selection of beverages depends on the event, the weather, the time of day, and your taste. For a party lasting about two hours, figure about half a bottle of wine, 8 ounces of liquor, 1 quart of beer, or 16 ounces of mixed punch per person. Plan on about 32 servings from a gallon of nonalcoholic punch. Expect each guest to use two glasses and have plenty of ice: one 5-pound bag for every four guests.

Surprises. Impromptu gatherings and unexpected guests can challenge even the most organized host. Take some of the surprise out of spur-of-the-moment occasions by keeping some of the following on hand: assorted crackers, pocket bread, and tortillas; canned salmon, crab, anchovies, smoked oysters, and tuna; canned green chiles; Cheddar, jack, and cream cheese; sour cream, plain yogurt, and mayonnaise; soy sauce; liquid hot pepper seasoning; and cocktail-size paper napkins.

Enjoy! Careful planning allows you the luxury of relaxing and enjoying the event. Easy to prepare, not overly time-consuming, and always delicious, our recipes will put you in a party mood.

A WORD ABOUT OUR NUTRITIONAL DATA

For our recipes, we provide a nutritional analysis stating calorie count; grams of protein, carbohydrates, and total fat; and milligrams of cholesterol and sodium. Generally, the analysis applies to a single serving, based on the number of servings given for each recipe and the amount of each ingredient. If a range is given for the number of servings and/or the amount of an ingredient, the analysis is based on an average of the figures given.

The nutritional analysis does not include optional ingredients or those for which no specific amount is stated. If an ingredient is listed with a substitution, the information was calculated using the first choice.

For a celebration of many cuisines, dip Water-crisped Tortilla Chips (recipe on page 16) in Mexico's Chile con Queso (recipe on page 8); serve the flavors of Italy on breadsticks, bell peppers, or cucumber slices with Pesto Cheese Spread (recipe on page 20); and enjoy a taste of southern France with Baked Vegetables Provençal (recipe on page 28).

6

DIPS & SPREADS

Popular with guests as well as with the cook, dips and spreads offer the maximum in versatility and taste with the minimum of fuss. Most are easily prepared with just a few ingredients and can be made well ahead of time. And all look attractive at the party without requiring a lot of attention.

Choose from an assortment of hot and cold presentations—creamy dips, meaty pâtés, and zesty vegetable spreads. Whether you serve them with crunchy vegetables, crisp crackers, slices of crusty bread, or chunks of fresh fruit, they're sure to disappear in minutes.

GORGONZOLA PESTO

Preparation time: About 10 minutes

Assertive pesto becomes even bolder when teamed with Gorgonzola. Serve this zesty appetizer surrounded by radicchio leaves and zucchini spears.

    3   cups lightly packed fresh basil
        leaves
    ⅔   cup (about 6 oz.) lightly packed
        crumbled Gorgonzola cheese
    ¼   cup olive oil
        Salt and pepper

In a blender or food processor, whirl basil, cheese, and oil until puréed. Transfer to a small bowl. Season to taste with salt and pepper.

If made ahead, cover and refrigerate until next day. Serve at room temperature. Makes about ¾ cup.

Per tablespoon: 101 calories, 4 g protein, 3 g carbohydrates, 9 g total fat, 11 mg cholesterol, 199 mg sodium

Pictured on page 6
CHILE CON QUESO

Preparation time: About 20 minutes
Cooking time: About 10 minutes

Offer this melted cheese dip with tortilla chips or colorful red or green bell pepper strips.

        Water-crisped Tortilla Chips or
        Fried Tortilla Chips (recipes on
        page 16), optional
    2   tablespoons salad oil
    1   medium-size onion, finely
        chopped
    1   can (4 oz.) diced green chiles
    ⅓   cup heavy cream
    1   cup (4 oz.) shredded Longhorn
        Cheddar cheese
        Red or green bell peppers,
        stemmed, seeded, and cut into
        ½-inch-wide strips (optional)

Prepare Fried Tortilla Chips, if desired; set aside.

Heat oil in a 3- to 4-quart pan over medium heat. Add onion and cook, stirring, until soft (about 7 minutes). Add chiles and cream; cook, stirring, until hot. Reduce heat and add cheese, stirring until melted.

Pour into a chafing or fondue dish over a low flame or into a dish on an electric warming tray set on low. Offer with bell pepper strips and chips, if desired. Makes 2 cups.

Per tablespoon: 32 calories, 1 g protein, .5 g carbohydrates, 3 g total fat, 7 mg cholesterol, 45 mg sodium

Pictured on front cover
RED PEPPER DIP

Preparation time: About 15 minutes
Cooking time: About 35 minutes

This colorful dip combines roasted red peppers, caramelized onions, and fresh thyme, showcasing them in a creamy ricotta and Parmesan cheese base. Good dippers include fresh vegetables, Cheese Wafers (recipe on page 42), and Polenta Triangles (recipe on page 44).

    3   tablespoons olive oil
    3   large onions, thinly sliced
    2   jars (7¼ oz. *each*) roasted red
        peppers
    2   teaspoons fresh thyme leaves or
        1 teaspoon dry thyme leaves
    2   tablespoons tomato paste
    ½   cup *each* grated Parmesan
        cheese and ricotta cheese
        Thyme sprigs (optional)

Heat oil in a wide frying pan over medium heat. Add onions and cook, stirring occasionally, until golden and very soft (about 30 minutes).

Add red peppers, thyme leaves, and tomato paste; cook, stirring, for 5 more minutes. Let cool briefly.

In a blender or food processor, whirl red pepper mixture, Parmesan, and ricotta until puréed. Transfer to a bowl and garnish with thyme sprigs, if desired.

If made ahead, cover and refrigerate until next day. Serve cold or at room temperature. Makes about 4 cups.

Per tablespoon: 16 calories, .6 g protein, 1 g carbohydrates, 1 g total fat, 1 mg cholesterol, 20 mg sodium

HERBED CHEESE DIP

Preparation time: About 10 minutes
Chilling time: At least 2 hours

Three kinds of cheese enrich this sour cream–based dip. Make it up to five days before serving; offer with raw green beans or celery sticks.

    1   cup sour cream
    1   small package (3 oz.) cream
        cheese, at room temperature
    ¼   cup (about 2 oz.) crumbled
        unripened goat cheese, such as
        Bûcheron
    ¾   teaspoon dill weed
    ¼   teaspoon *each* dry sage, dry
        basil, and dry thyme leaves
    ¼   teaspoon freshly ground pepper
    1   clove garlic, minced or pressed
    ⅓   cup (3 oz.) crumbled blue-
        veined cheese

Beat sour cream, cream cheese, goat cheese, dill, sage, basil, thyme, pepper, and garlic until smooth and well blended. Stir in blue-veined cheese. Cover and refrigerate for at least 2 hours or up to 5 days. Makes about 1¾ cups.

Per tablespoon: 47 calories, 1 g protein, .7 g carbohydrates, 4 g total fat, 11 mg cholesterol, 68 mg sodium

CREAMY CRAB DIP

Preparation time: About 10 minutes

Spoon this luscious crabmeat dip into the centers of cold cooked artichokes for an impressive appetizer.

- 1 large package (8 oz.) cream cheese, at room temperature
- 2 tablespoons *each* dry white wine and lemon juice
- 1 clove garlic, minced or pressed
- 1 teaspoon Dijon mustard
- ½ teaspoon Worcestershire
- ¼ cup thinly sliced green onions (including tops)
- ½ pound crabmeat
  Salt and pepper

Beat cream cheese, wine, lemon juice, garlic, mustard, and Worcestershire until blended. Stir in onions and crab. Season to taste with salt and pepper. If made ahead, cover and refrigerate until next day. Makes about 2 cups.

Per tablespoon: 33 calories, 2 g protein, .3 g carbohydrates, 3 g total fat, 15 mg cholesterol, 47 mg sodium

SMOKED SALMON DIP

Preparation time: About 10 minutes

Accented with dill and onion, this creamy dip is an elegant starter. Endive spears are the perfect accompaniment for dipping.

- 1 large package (8 oz.) cream cheese, at room temperature
- ⅓ cup (about 3 oz.) chopped smoked salmon or lox
- ¼ cup sour cream
- 1 tablespoon *each* lime juice and minced onion
- 3 tablespoons chopped fresh dill or 2 teaspoons dill weed
  Dill sprigs (optional)
  Endive spears, washed and crisped (optional)

Beat cream cheese, salmon, sour cream, lime juice, and onion until well blended and fluffy. Mix in chopped dill. Transfer to a small bowl. If made ahead, cover and refrigerate for up to 3 days. Serve at room temperature.

If desired, garnish with dill sprigs and surround with endive. Makes about 1 cup.

Per tablespoon: 64 calories, 2 g protein, .7 g carbohydrates, 6 g total fat, 18 mg cholesterol, 86 mg sodium

CURRY-YOGURT DIP

Preparation time: About 10 minutes
Standing time: About 30 minutes

Tiny cooked shrimp are mixed with shredded zucchini in this light curry and yogurt combination. Make the dip just before serving and offer it with an assortment of raw vegetables.

- 1 small zucchini (about 3 oz.), shredded
  About 1 teaspoon salt
- 1 cup plain yogurt
- ½ teaspoon curry powder
- ¼ cup thinly sliced green onions (including tops)
- ½ pound small cooked shrimp
- ¼ cup chopped cilantro (coriander)
  Ground red pepper (cayenne)

Mix zucchini with 1 teaspoon of the salt. Let stand until zucchini is limp and liquid has drained from it (about 30 minutes). Rinse and drain, squeezing out as much water as possible.

Gently mix zucchini, yogurt, curry powder, onions, shrimp, and cilantro; season to taste with salt and pepper. Pour mixture into a bowl. Sprinkle with additional pepper, if desired. Makes 2⅓ cups.

Per tablespoon: 11 calories, 2 g protein, .5 g carbohydrates, .2 g total fat, 12 mg cholesterol, 33 mg sodium

DILL DIP

Preparation time: About 5 minutes
Chilling time: At least 4 hours

You can make this easy dill-accented dip with ingredients you have on hand. Cherry tomatoes, celery sticks, and cauliflowerets are the perfect partners.

- ⅔ cup *each* mayonnaise and sour cream
- 2 tablespoons chopped parsley
- 2½ teaspoons *each* dill weed and finely chopped onion

Mix mayonnaise and sour cream. Stir in parsley, dill, and onion until well blended. Cover and refrigerate for at least 4 hours or until next day. Makes about 1⅓ cups.

Per tablespoon: 67 calories, .3 g protein, .6 g carbohydrates, 7 g total fat, 7 mg cholesterol, 44 mg sodium

HORSERADISH DIP

Preparation time: About 5 minutes
Chilling time: At least 1 hour

This dip can do double duty at a barbecue. You can serve it with crisp, raw vegetables, such as jicama and cucumber, and offer it as a dipping sauce for grilled beef.

- 2 cups plain yogurt
- ¼ cup minced green onions (including tops)
- ½ teaspoon *each* mustard seeds and cumin seeds
- 1 to 2 tablespoons prepared horseradish

Stir together yogurt, onions, mustard seeds, cumin seeds, and horseradish. Cover and refrigerate for at least 1 hour or up to 3 days. Makes about 2½ cups.

Per tablespoon: 8 calories, .6 g protein, .9 g carbohydrates, .2 g total fat, .7 mg cholesterol, 9 mg sodium

Pictured on page 62

MINT SAUCE

◆

Preparation time: About 15 minutes
Cooking time: About 30 seconds

Summertime parties call for a cool, refreshing dip like this one. Crisp, bright green pea pods complement the minty sour cream sauce in color, flavor, and texture.

- 1 **pound Chinese pea pods (snow or sugar peas), ends and strings removed (optional)**
- ¼ **cup *each* sour cream and mayonnaise**
- 2 **tablespoons coarsely chopped fresh mint leaves**

In a wide frying pan, cook peas, if used, in 2 inches boiling water just until bright green (about 30 seconds). Drain, immerse in ice water, and drain again. Set aside.

In a blender or food processor, whirl sour cream, mayonnaise, and mint until mint is finely chopped. Transfer to a small bowl and arrange on a platter with peas, if used. Makes about ½ cup.

Per tablespoon: 65 calories, .3 g protein, .5 g carbohydrates, 7 g total fat, 7 mg cholesterol, 43 mg sodium

SPRING ASPARAGUS DIP

◆

Preparation time: About 10 minutes
Cooking time: About 2 minutes

Announce a special springtime event with this pale green vegetable dip. Accompany with red and yellow bell pepper strips for extra color and crunch.

- 1 **pound asparagus**
- 1 **green onion (including top), thinly sliced**
- 2 **tablespoons water**
- 1 **tablespoon salad oil**
- 1 **small package (3 oz.) cream cheese, at room temperature**
- ½ **cup sour cream**
- 1 **teaspoon lemon juice**
  Salt and pepper

Snap off and discard tough ends of asparagus; peel stalks, if desired. Cut asparagus into thin slices.

Combine asparagus, onion, water, and oil in a wide frying pan. Cover and cook over medium-high heat, stirring occasionally, until asparagus is tender crisp (about 2 minutes). Uncover and let cool briefly.

In a blender or food processor, whirl asparagus mixture, cream cheese, sour cream, and lemon juice until well blended. Season to taste with salt and pepper. Makes about 1½ cups.

Per tablespoon: 30 calories, .7 g protein, .7 g carbohydrates, 3 g total fat, 6 mg cholesterol, 13 mg sodium

SPINACH DIP

Preparation time: About 5 minutes
Chilling time: At least 2 hours

This simple dip can be put together in minutes and taken from the refrigerator when company comes. Serve with turnip slices, red bell pepper strips, and other raw vegetables.

- 1 **cup chopped cooked spinach or 1 package (10 oz.) frozen chopped spinach, thawed**
- ⅓ **cup coarsely chopped green onions (including tops)**
- ½ **cup lightly packed parsley sprigs**
- 1 **tablespoon lemon juice**
- 1 **cup sour cream**
- 1½ **teaspoons pepper**
- 2 **cloves garlic, minced or pressed Salt**

If using frozen spinach, drain well, squeezing out as much liquid as possible. Place spinach in a blender or food processor with onions, parsley, lemon juice, sour cream, pepper, and garlic. Whirl until blended. Season to taste with salt. Cover and refrigerate for at least 2 hours or until next day. Makes 2 cups.

Per tablespoon: 18 calories, .4 g protein, .8 g carbohydrates, 2 g total fat, 3 mg cholesterol, 8 mg sodium

Pictured on facing page

TARRAGON MAYONNAISE

◆

Preparation time: About 5 minutes

Fresh tarragon imparts a pungent flavor to this creamy herbed mayonnaise. You can make it up to two weeks before serving; offer it with crisp radishes and firm mushrooms.

- 1 **egg**
- 1 **tablespoon *each* Dijon mustard and tarragon vinegar**
- 2 **teaspoons lemon juice**
- 2 **tablespoons chopped fresh tarragon leaves or 1 teaspoon dry tarragon leaves**
- ¼ **teaspoon ground white pepper**
- ¾ **cup salad oil**
- ¼ **cup olive oil**
  Salt
  Tarragon sprigs (optional)

In a blender or food processor, whirl egg, mustard, vinegar, lemon juice, chopped tarragon, and pepper until well blended. Combine salad oil and olive oil. With motor running, add oil mixture, a few drops at a time at first, increasing to a slow, steady stream as mixture thickens. Season to taste with salt. If made ahead, cover and refrigerate for up to 2 weeks.

Transfer to a bowl. Garnish with tarragon sprigs, if desired. Makes about 1⅓ cups.

Per tablespoon: 96 calories, .3 g protein, .2 g carbohydrates, 11 g total fat, 10 mg cholesterol, 25 mg sodium

Autumn is the perfect time to offer herb-rich Tarragon Mayonnaise (recipe on facing page) and sweet-tart Apple Aïoli (recipe on page 12). Toast the harvest with Mulled Apple-Ginger Sparkler (recipe on page 89).

PIMENTO AÏOLI

Preparation time: About 5 minutes

Pimentos lend fiery orange color to this garlicky mayonnaise. Crisp, pale endive spears offer complementary taste, texture, and color.

- 1 jar (4 oz.) sliced pimentos, drained
- 1 large clove garlic
- ½ teaspoon dry mustard
- 2 teaspoons white wine vinegar
- 1 egg yolk
- ⅓ cup *each* olive and salad oil
  Salt

In a blender or food processor, whirl pimentos, garlic, mustard, vinegar, and egg yolk until blended. Combine olive oil and salad oil. With motor running, add oil mixture, a few drops at a time at first, increasing to a slow, steady stream as mixture thickens. Season to taste with salt. If made ahead, cover and refrigerate for up to 3 days. Makes about 1 cup.

Per tablespoon: 85 calories, .3 g protein, .5 g carbohydrates, 9 g total fat, 13 mg cholesterol, 2 mg sodium

Pictured on page 11
APPLE AÏOLI

Preparation time: About 5 minutes

Adding apple juice and lemon juice to aïoli gives the garlic dip a sweet-sour accent. Perfect for an autumn party, the dip is good with sliced pears and apples as well as with fresh vegetables.

- 3 tablespoons lemon juice
- 2 tablespoons thawed frozen apple juice concentrate
- 2 egg yolks
- 1 clove garlic, minced or pressed
  About ½ teaspoon ground cinnamon
- 1 cup salad oil

In a blender or food processor, whirl lemon juice, apple juice concentrate, egg yolks, garlic, and ½ teaspoon of the cinnamon until blended. With motor running, add oil, a few drops at a time at first, increasing to a slow, steady stream as mixture thickens.

Transfer to a bowl and sprinkle with additional cinnamon, if desired. Makes 1⅓ cups.

Per tablespoon: 101 calories, .3 g protein, .9 g carbohydrates, 11 g total fat, 20 mg cholesterol, 2 mg sodium

HOLLANDAISE

Preparation time: About 5 minutes
Cooking time: About 4 minutes

This quickly made hollandaise is delicious with crisp vegetables.

- 3 egg yolks, at room temperature
- 1½ tablespoons lemon juice
- ⅛ teaspoon ground red pepper (cayenne)
- 1 teaspoon Dijon mustard
- 1 cup (½ lb.) butter or margarine
  Salt

In a blender or food processor, whirl egg yolks, lemon juice, pepper, and mustard until blended; set aside. In a 1-quart pan, melt butter over medium heat until bubbling (do not let butter brown). With motor running, add butter to yolk mixture, a few drops at a time at first, increasing to a slow, steady stream as mixture thickens. Season to taste with salt. Makes about 1½ cups.

Per tablespoon: 76 calories, .4 g protein, .1 g carbohydrates, 8 g total fat, 47 mg cholesterol, 85 mg sodium

Hollandaise with Cucumber

Follow directions for **Hollandaise.** After seasoning, stir in 1 tablespoon *each* chopped **parsley** and **chives** and 1 small **cucumber,** peeled, seeded, and chopped. Makes about 2 cups.

Per tablespoon: 57 calories, .3 g protein, .2 g carbohydrates, 6 g total fat, 35 mg cholesterol, 64 mg sodium

TOASTED ALMOND MAYONNAISE

Preparation time: About 5 minutes
Cooking time: About 8 minutes

Take advantage of summer's bounty by offering baby vegetables, such as corn, carrots, and bok choy, with this rich mayonnaise. Toasted almonds add flavor to the egg yolk–based dip.

- Ground Toasted Almonds (recipe follows)
- 2 egg yolks
- 2 cloves garlic, minced or pressed
- 1½ tablespoons lemon juice
- ½ teaspoon sugar
- 1 to 4 tablespoons dry white wine
- 1 cup olive or salad oil
  Salt

Prepare Ground Toasted Almonds; set aside.

In a blender or food processor, whirl egg yolks, garlic, lemon juice, sugar, and 1 tablespoon of the wine until blended. With motor running, add oil, a few drops at a time at first, increasing to a slow, steady stream as mixture thickens. Stir in almonds. For a thinner consistency, add more wine. Season to taste with salt.

If made ahead, cover and refrigerate for up to 2 days. Makes 1½ cups.

Ground Toasted Almonds.
Spread ⅓ cup whole **unblanched almonds** in a 9- to 10-inch baking pan and bake in a 350° oven until golden under skin (about 8 minutes). Let cool. Whirl in a blender or food processor until finely ground.

Per tablespoon: 97 calories, .6 g protein, .6 g carbohydrates, 10 g total fat, 18 mg cholesterol, 1 mg sodium

BAGNA CAUDA

Preparation time: About 25 minutes
Cooking time: About 5 minutes

This northern Italian anchovy butter sauce (pronounced BAHN-yah COW-dah) contains more than a hint of garlic. Use it as a dip for fresh vegetables and crunchy bread.

- 1 cup (½ lb.) butter or margarine
- ½ cup olive oil
- 5 large cloves garlic, minced or pressed
- 2 tablespoons lemon juice
- 1½ teaspoons pepper
- 2 cans (2 oz. *each*) anchovy fillets

Heat butter, oil, garlic, lemon juice, and pepper in a 3- to 4-cup heatproof container over medium heat. Drain oil from anchovies into butter mixture; finely chop anchovies and stir into sauce.

Keep warm over a candle or alcohol flame, or reheat periodically; sauce may brown slightly, but do not let butter burn. Makes about 2 cups.

Per tablespoon: 94 calories, .9 g protein, .3 g carbohydrates, 10 g total fat, 17 mg cholesterol, 162 mg sodium

FISH ROE DIP

Preparation time: About 10 minutes
Chilling time: At least 2 hours

Red caviar is the key ingredient in this version of the Greek dip *taramasalata*. Crusty bread cubes and cucumber or zucchini slices are good scoopers.

- 4 sandwich-size slices white bread, crusts trimmed
- 1 small onion, grated
- 1 jar (4 oz.) red caviar, such as carp roe or red whitefish caviar, or 1 tube (about 3.3 oz.) red smoked carp roe paste
- ¼ cup lemon juice
- ½ cup *each* olive and salad oil

Soak bread in water to cover for 5 minutes; squeeze dry. In a blender or food processor, whirl bread, onion, caviar, and lemon juice until smooth. Combine olive oil and salad oil. With motor running, gradually add oil mixture, a few drops at a time at first, increasing to a slow, steady stream as mixture thickens. Cover and refrigerate for at least 2 hours or until next day. Makes 2 cups.

Per tablespoon: 77 calories, 1 g protein, 2 g carbohydrates, 7 g total fat, 21 mg cholesterol, 68 mg sodium

ASIAN EGGPLANT DIP

Preparation time: About 10 minutes
Cooking time: About 1 hour

Not for the timid, this eggplant purée is boldly seasoned with ginger, garlic, sesame oil, and chile. Serve on paper-thin crackers.

- 1 large eggplant (about 1½ lbs.), ends trimmed
- 2 cloves garlic
- 2 tablespoons soy sauce
- 2 tablespoons rice wine (mirin) or dry vermouth
- 1 tablespoon *each* minced fresh ginger, minced cilantro (coriander), and sesame oil
- ½ teaspoon crushed dried hot red chiles
  Salt

With a fork, pierce eggplant deeply in 10 to 12 places. Set in an 8- to 9-inch baking pan. Bake in a 350° oven until very soft when pressed (about 1 hour). Let cool. If desired, trim off and discard skin. Cut eggplant into large chunks.

Place eggplant, garlic, soy, wine, ginger, cilantro, oil, and chiles in a blender or food processor and whirl until fairly smooth; scrape container sides often. Season to taste with salt.

If made ahead, cover and refrigerate for up to 4 days. Serve at room temperature. Makes about 2 cups.

Per tablespoon: 13 calories, .3 g protein, 2 g carbohydrates, .4 g total fat, 0 mg cholesterol, 65 mg sodium

MOROCCAN EGGPLANT DIP

Preparation time: About 10 minutes
Cooking time: About 25 minutes
Chilling time: At least 2 hours

This versatile dip can be scooped on pumpernickel bread or served with fresh vegetables.

- 3 tablespoons olive oil
- 1 large eggplant (about 1½ lbs.), ends trimmed, diced
- 1 can (8 oz.) tomato sauce
- 2 cloves garlic, minced or pressed
- 1 large green bell pepper, stemmed, seeded, and chopped
- 1 tablespoon ground cumin
- ¼ teaspoon ground red pepper (cayenne)
- 2 teaspoons *each* sugar and salt
- ¼ cup red wine vinegar
- ¼ cup chopped cilantro (coriander)

Heat oil in a wide frying pan over medium heat. Add eggplant, tomato sauce, garlic, bell pepper, cumin, red pepper, sugar, salt, and vinegar. Cover and cook over medium heat for 20 minutes. Uncover, increase heat to high, and boil, stirring, until reduced to about 3 cups (about 5 more minutes). Let cool; then cover and refrigerate for at least 2 hours or until next day. Just before serving, stir in cilantro. Makes 3 cups.

Per tablespoon: 15 calories, .2 g protein, 2 g carbohydrates, .9 g total fat, 0 mg cholesterol, 121 mg sodium

Layer sour cream, green onions, bell peppers, and jack cheese over Guacamole (recipe on facing page) and easy-to-prepare Black Bean Dip (recipe on facing page); scoop up the Southwestern specialty with crisp jicama slices.

HUMMUS

Preparation time: About 5 minutes
Cooking time: About 3 minutes

This garlic-rich garbanzo dip can be made in minutes and is perfect at a barbecue. Offer Pita Crisps (recipe on page 16) with this Middle Eastern treat.

¼ cup sesame seeds
1 can (15 oz.) garbanzo beans, drained (reserve liquid)
4 tablespoons olive oil
3 tablespoons lemon juice
2 cloves garlic
   Salt and pepper

In a small frying pan, toast sesame seeds over medium heat, shaking pan often, until golden (about 3 minutes). Transfer seeds to a blender or food processor and add garbanzos, 2 tablespoons of the oil, lemon juice, garlic, and 6 tablespoons of the reserved garbanzo liquid. Whirl, adding more liquid if needed, until hummus is smooth but still thick enough to hold its shape. Season to taste with salt and pepper.

Transfer hummus to a shallow bowl. Drizzle with remaining 2 tablespoons oil. Makes 2 cups.

Per tablespoon: 38 calories, .9 g protein, 3 g carbohydrates, 2 g total fat, 0 mg cholesterol, 40 mg sodium

LAYERED KIDNEY BEAN DIP

Preparation time: About 15 minutes
Cooking time: About 4 minutes

You can build this multitiered dip quickly with marinated artichoke hearts and canned kidney beans. Let guests scoop up the dip with crisp celery sticks or Garlic Toast (recipe on page 16).

2 teaspoons olive oil
1 clove garlic, minced or pressed
2 ounces prosciutto, chopped
1 tablespoon red wine vinegar
1 can (15½ oz.) kidney beans, drained (reserve liquid)
1 tablespoon minced fresh basil leaves
⅛ teaspoon pepper
1 jar (about 6 oz.) marinated artichoke hearts, drained and cut in half
1 cup (4 oz.) shredded provolone cheese

Heat oil in a small frying pan over medium-high heat. Add garlic and prosciutto and cook, stirring, until prosciutto is crisp (about 4 minutes). Add vinegar and let cool.

In a large bowl, mash beans. Stir in ¼ cup of the reserved liquid from beans, prosciutto, basil, and pepper. Mound on a plate. Top with artichokes and sprinkle with cheese. Makes about 8 servings.

Per serving: 139 calories, 8 g protein, 11 g carbohydrates, 7 g total fat, 14 mg cholesterol, 567 mg sodium

Pictured on facing page

BLACK BEAN DIP

Preparation time: About 25 minutes
Cooking time: About 8 minutes

Serve this layered dip with jicama or tortilla chips (recipes on page 16).

1⅔ cups Guacamole (recipe at right)
6 slices bacon, coarsely chopped
1 small onion, chopped
½ teaspoon chili powder
1 can (15 oz.) black beans, drained (reserve ⅓ cup of the liquid)
1 cup (4 oz.) shredded jack cheese
1 *each* small red and yellow bell peppers (or 2 of either), stemmed, seeded, and chopped
¼ cup thinly sliced green onions (including tops)
   Jicama, peeled and cut into triangles (optional)
   Sour cream, cilantro (coriander) sprigs, and jalapeño chiles (optional)

Prepare Guacamole; set aside.

In an 8- to 10-inch frying pan, cook bacon, chopped onion, and chili powder over medium heat, stirring occasionally, until bacon is crisp (about 8 minutes). Drain and discard fat. Let cool.

In a large bowl, coarsely mash beans. Stir in reserved liquid and bacon mixture. Mound in center of a large plate; top with Guacamole. Sprinkle with cheese, bell peppers, and green onions. If desired, arrange jicama around edge and garnish dip with sour cream, cilantro, and chiles. Makes about 8 servings.

Per serving: 247 calories, 10 g protein, 18 g carbohydrates, 16 g total fat, 16 mg cholesterol, 534 mg sodium

Pictured on facing page

GUACAMOLE

Preparation time: About 10 minutes

Be sure to choose ripe, buttery avocados for this popular dip.

2 large ripe avocados
2 to 3 tablespoons lemon or lime juice
1 clove garlic, minced or pressed
1 to 2 tablespoons chopped cilantro (coriander)
2 to 4 canned green chiles, seeded and chopped
1 medium-size tomato, peeled, seeded, and chopped
   Minced jalapeño or serrano chiles (optional)
   Salt
   Cilantro (coriander) sprigs (optional)

Pit avocados and scoop out pulp; mash coarsely with a fork. Stir in lemon juice, garlic, chopped cilantro, green chiles, and tomato. Add jalapeño chiles to taste, if desired. Season to taste with salt.

Spoon into a bowl. Garnish with cilantro sprigs, if desired. Makes about 1⅔ cups.

Per tablespoon: 33 calories, .5 g protein, 2 g carbohydrates, 3 g total fat, 0 mg cholesterol, 52 mg sodium

Here's a simple way to add a special touch to a party with a minimum of fuss. Starting with purchased bread, corn tortillas, or even won ton skins, you can create savory toast rounds, crisp chips, or golden "crackers" to serve as holders for your favorite dips and spreads.

FRIED TORTILLA CHIPS

Preparation time: About 5 minutes
Cooking time: About 10 minutes

These all-purpose chips are the perfect scoop for Guacamole (recipe on page 15) or Salsa Fresca (recipe on facing page). For less fat, use our water-crisped variation.

- 12 corn tortillas (6-in. diameter)
  Salad oil
  Salt

Stack tortillas and cut into 6 wedges. In a deep 3- to 4-quart pan, heat about 1½ inches oil to 350°F on a deep-frying thermometer. Add tortillas, a batch at a time, and cook, turning occasionally, until crisp (about 30 seconds). Drain on paper towels. Season to taste with salt.

If made ahead, store in an airtight container for up to 2 days. Makes 6 dozen scoops.

Per scoop: 21 calories, .4 g protein, 2 g carbohydrates, 1 g total fat, 0 mg cholesterol, 9 mg sodium

Pictured on page 6
Water-crisped Tortilla Chips

Immerse 12 **corn tortillas** (6-in. diameter), one at a time, in water; drain briefly. Season to taste with **salt.** Stack and cut into 6 wedges. Arrange in a single layer on baking sheets. Bake in a 500° oven for 4 minutes. Turn and continue baking until crisp (about 1 more minute).

SIMPLE SCOOPS

If made ahead, store in an airtight container for up to 2 weeks. Makes 6 dozen scoops.

Per scoop: 11 calories, .4 g protein, 2 g carbohydrates, .2 g total fat, 0 mg cholesterol, 9 mg sodium

Pictured on page 19
GARLIC TOAST

Preparation time: About 5 minutes
Cooking time: About 3 minutes

Baguette slices brushed with garlic-flavored oil complement Prosciutto-topped Brie (recipe on page 18) and other spreads.

- 1 clove garlic, minced or pressed
- ¼ cup olive oil
- 2 teaspoons finely chopped fresh oregano leaves or 1 teaspoon dry oregano leaves
- 1 small French baguette (8 oz.), sliced ¼ inch thick

Mix garlic, oil, and oregano; set aside.

Place bread slices in a single layer on baking sheets. Broil about 4 inches below heat until golden (about 2 minutes). Remove from oven, turn, and brush tops with garlic mixture. Return to oven and continue broiling until lightly browned (about 1 more minute). Serve warm or at room temperature. Makes 2 dozen scoops.

Per scoop: 48 calories, .9 g protein, 5 g carbohydrates, 3 g total fat, .3 mg cholesterol, 55 mg sodium

PITA CRISPS

Preparation time: About 5 minutes
Cooking time: About 5 minutes

These crispy triangles are perfect with Hummus (recipe on page 15).

- 6 pocket bread rounds (6-in. diameter)
- 1 clove garlic, minced or pressed
- ¼ cup olive oil
  Salt and pepper

Split pocket breads to make 12 rounds. Combine garlic and oil and brush mixture over split sides. Season to taste with salt and pepper. Stack and cut into 6 to 8 wedges. Place in a single layer on baking sheets and bake in a 400° oven until crisp and golden (about 5 minutes). Makes 6 to 8 dozen scoops.

Per scoop: 18 calories, .4 g protein, 3 g carbohydrates, .7 g total fat, 0 mg cholesterol, 26 mg sodium

WON TON CRISPIES

Preparation time: About 5 minutes
Cooking time: About 10 minutes

Try this crisp cracker with Fresh Mushroom Pâté (recipe on page 28).

- 4 tablespoons butter or margarine, melted
- 20 won ton skins
- ½ cup grated Parmesan cheese

Brush 2 baking sheets with 1 tablespoon of the butter. Cut won ton skins in half; place about half the skins in a single layer on baking sheets. Brush with 1 more tablespoon butter; sprinkle with half the cheese. Bake in a 375° oven until golden (about 5 minutes). Repeat with remaining skins. Makes 40 scoops.

Per scoop: 25 calories, 1 g protein, 2 g carbohydrates, 2 g total fat, 4 mg cholesterol, 39 mg sodium

TROPICAL FRUIT SALSA

Preparation time: About 15 minutes

Fresh mango, pineapple, and honey-dew are mixed into a colorful mélange enlivened with red pepper and cilantro. The dip can be stored for up to 2 days; it's delicious with barbecued chicken.

- 1 **firm-ripe mango, peeled and diced**
- 1 **cup *each* diced fresh pineapple and diced honeydew**
- ½ **cup diced red bell pepper**
- ⅓ **cup seasoned rice wine vinegar**
- 2 **tablespoons minced cilantro (coriander)**
- ½ **teaspoon crushed red pepper flakes**

Mix mango, pineapple, honeydew, bell pepper, vinegar, cilantro, and red pepper flakes. If made ahead, cover and refrigerate for up to 2 days. Makes 3½ cups.

Per tablespoon: 6 calories, 0 g protein, 2 g carbohydrates, 0 g total fat, 0 mg cholesterol, .7 mg sodium

TOMATILLO SALSA

Preparation time: About 20 minutes
Cooking time: About 15 minutes

Tomatillos combined with lime juice and chicken broth create a tangy alternative to traditional fresh salsa. Serve with thin slices of apple or jicama.

- 1¼ **pounds tomatillos, husks removed**
- ⅓ **cup chopped cilantro (coriander)**
- 1 **jalapeño or other small hot chile, stemmed**
- ¾ **cup regular-strength chicken broth**
- ⅓ **cup lime juice**
  Salt

Rinse tomatillos. Arrange in a single layer on a baking sheet and bake in a 500° oven until slightly singed (about 15 minutes). Let cool.

In a blender or food processor, whirl tomatillos with cilantro and chile; stir in broth and lime juice. Season to taste with salt. If made ahead, cover and refrigerate for up to 2 days. Makes 3 cups.

Per tablespoon: 4 calories, .2 g protein, .6 g carbohydrates, .1 g total fat, 0 mg cholesterol, 16 mg sodium

SALSA FRESCA

Preparation time: About 10 minutes

It takes next to no time to make this classic Mexican condiment in the blender, but for a drier, chunkier texture, try making it by hand.

- 2 **cloves garlic**
- ½ **medium-size onion, quartered**
- 1 **or 2 jalapeño or other small hot chiles, stemmed and seeded**
- ¼ **cup lightly packed cilantro (coriander)**
- 1 **pound firm-ripe tomatoes, seeded**
- 2 **tablespoons salad oil**
  Juice of 1 lime
  Salt and pepper

To make in a blender or food processor: Whirl garlic, onion, chiles, cilantro, and tomatoes in a blender or food processor just until coarsely chopped. Add oil and lime juice; whirl until finely chopped. Season to taste with salt and pepper.

To make by hand: Using a sharp knife, mince garlic, onion, and chiles.

Finely chop cilantro and dice tomatoes. Combine in a nonmetallic bowl; add oil and lime juice. Season to taste with salt and pepper.

If made ahead, cover and refrigerate for up to 2 days. Makes 2 cups.

Per tablespoon: 11 calories, .1 g protein, .9 g carbohydrates, .9 g total fat, 0 mg cholesterol, 1 mg sodium

TOMATO RELISH

Preparation time: About 10 minutes
Cooking time: About 15 minutes

Blend tomatoes with fresh ginger, garlic, onion, and turmeric for an easy-to-prepare dip with an Asian accent. Serve with cucumber slices.

- 2 **to 4 small dried hot red chiles, stemmed and seeded**
- 2 **tablespoons water**
- 1 **large onion, quartered**
- 4 **cloves garlic**
- 2 **teaspoons chopped fresh ginger**
- 2 **tablespoons salad oil**
- ¼ **teaspoon turmeric**
- 1 **large can (28 oz.) tomatoes, drained**

In a blender or food processor, whirl chiles, water, onion, garlic, and ginger until puréed.

Heat oil in a wide frying pan over medium heat. Add onion mixture and turmeric and cook, stirring, until liquid has evaporated (about 5 minutes). Remove from heat.

Whirl tomatoes in blender until puréed. Add to onion mixture and cook, stirring occasionally, until reduced to about 2 cups (about 10 minutes). Serve at room temperature. Makes about 2 cups.

Per tablespoon: 15 calories, .3 g protein, 2 g carbohydrates, .9 g total fat, 0 mg cholesterol, 41 mg sodium

FETA CHEESE SPREAD

◆

Preparation time: About 5 minutes

Nothing could be simpler, or tastier, than this three-ingredient cheese spread. Offer it with crusty Italian bread and prosciutto.

- **8 ounces feta cheese, crumbled**
- **2 large packages (8 oz. *each*) cream cheese, at room temperature**
- **½ cup whipping cream**

Beat feta and cream cheese until blended. Stir in cream. If made ahead, cover and refrigerate for up to 5 days. Makes about 2½ cups.

Per tablespoon: 63 calories, 2 g protein, .6 g carbohydrates, 6 g total fat, 21 mg cholesterol, 98 mg sodium

MELTED BRIE IN CRUST

◆

Preparation time: About 15 minutes
Cooking time: About 20 minutes

Bake Brie in a loaf of bread; then watch both the melted cheese and the container disappear.

- **1 round or oval loaf French bread (about 1 lb.)**
- **⅓ cup olive oil or melted butter**
- **2 cloves garlic, minced or pressed**
- **1 to 1½ pounds ripe Brie, Camembert, or St. André cheese, rind trimmed, if desired**

Using a serrated knife and your fingers, remove center of bread in a single piece, leaving a shell about ½ inch thick on sides and bottom. Around rim of shell, make 1½-inch-deep cuts about 1½ inches apart. Cut bread pulled from loaf into 1½- by 2-inch chunks about ½ inch thick.

Mix oil and garlic. Brush inside of shell with about 3 tablespoons of the oil mixture; brush bread chunks with remaining mixture.

Cut cheese into chunks and place in bread shell. Place filled shell and bread chunks in a single layer on two 10- by 15-inch baking sheets. Bake in a 350° oven for 10 minutes. Remove bread chunks and let cool on a wire rack. Continue baking filled shell until cheese is melted (about 10 more minutes).

Place shell on a serving board; surround with toasted bread chunks. Makes about 1 dozen servings.

Per serving: 321 calories, 13 g protein, 21 g carbohydrates, 20 g total fat, 48 mg cholesterol, 517 mg sodium

MELTED BRIE WITH WINTER FRUITS

◆

Preparation time: About 15 minutes
Soaking time: About 2 hours
Cooking time: About 25 minutes

A mixture of dried and fresh fruits soaked in wine is tucked into a round of Brie and then baked. Serve the elegant spread on toasted baguette slices.

- **¾ cup chopped pitted dates**
- **1 *each* small apple and small firm-ripe pear, peeled, cored, and diced**
- **½ cup *each* currants and chopped pecans**
- **⅓ cup rosé wine or apple juice**
- **1 whole firm-ripe Brie cheese (2 lbs.), chilled**

Mix dates, apple, pear, currants, pecans, and wine. Set aside until fruit is softened (about 2 hours).

Cut cheese in half crosswise. Place a portion, cut side up, in a greased shallow baking dish just slightly larger than cheese. Spread with 2¼ cups of the fruit mixture. Cover with remaining cheese, cut side down. Spoon remaining fruit onto center of

cheese. (At this point, you may cover and refrigerate for up to 2 days.)

Bake, uncovered, in a 350° oven until cheese is melted at edges and warm in center (about 25 minutes). Makes about 16 servings.

Per serving: 256 calories, 12 g protein, 13 g carbohydrates, 18 g total fat, 57 mg cholesterol, 358 mg sodium

Pictured on facing page

PROSCIUTTO-TOPPED BRIE

◆

Preparation time: About 10 minutes
Cooking time: About 12 minutes

There's a surprise hidden in this hot cheese spread: a layer of sun-dried tomatoes. Offer the baked Brie with celery sticks and garlicky French bread slices.

- **1 whole firm-ripe Brie cheese (8 oz.), chilled**
- **3 tablespoons finely chopped dried tomatoes packed in oil, drained (reserve oil)**
- **1 ounce thinly sliced prosciutto, slivered**

Cut cheese in half crosswise. Place a portion, cut side up, in a greased shallow baking dish just slightly larger than cheese. Spread with tomatoes. Cover with remaining cheese, cut side down. Mix prosciutto with 1 tablespoon of the reserved oil from tomatoes and mound over cheese. (At this point, you may cover and refrigerate until next day.)

Bake, uncovered, in a 350° oven until cheese is melted at edges and warm in center (about 12 minutes). Makes about 4 servings.

Per serving: 268 calories, 13 g protein, 2 g carbohydrates, 23 g total fat, 61 mg cholesterol, 742 mg sodium

Hot and cold cheese spreads are crowd pleasers.
Stuffed Camembert (recipe on page 20), filled with a
variety of cheeses and onions, and Prosciutto-topped
Brie (recipe on facing page), stuffed with dried tomatoes,
will disappear on crackers, celery, and Garlic Toast
(recipe on page 16).

LAZY LIPTAUER CHEESE

Preparation time: About 5 minutes

This version of the famous Austro-Hungarian cheese spread is made with a few shortcuts. The creamy blend is best served on dense-textured pumpernickel bread and topped with crisp dill pickle slices.

- 1 cup small curd cottage cheese
- 1 small package (3 oz.) cream cheese, at room temperature
- 2 teaspoons paprika
- 1 teaspoon *each* dry mustard and caraway seeds

Beat cottage cheese, cream cheese, paprika, mustard, and caraway seeds until smoothly blended. If made ahead, cover and refrigerate for up to 2 days. Makes about 1¼ cups.

Per tablespoon: 28 calories, 2 g protein, .6 g carbohydrates, 2 g total fat, 6 mg cholesterol, 59 mg sodium

WALNUT CHEESE SPREAD

Preparation time: About 10 minutes
Cooking time: About 8 minutes
Chilling time: At least 2 hours

Toasted walnuts add texture as well as flavor to this cream cheese and olive spread. You can make it up to 2 days in advance; serve with Pita Crisps (recipe on page 16).

- ½ cup chopped walnuts
- 10 pimento-stuffed green olives
- 1 large package (8 oz.) cream cheese, at room temperature
- 2 teaspoons liquid from olives
- 4 green onions (including tops), chopped

Spread walnuts in a shallow baking pan. Bake in a 350° oven until lightly browned (about 8 minutes). Let cool briefly.

Meanwhile, finely chop olives. Beat cream cheese with olive liquid until fluffy. Stir in nuts, olives, and onions. Cover and refrigerate for at least 2 hours or up to 2 days. Makes 1½ cups.

Per tablespoon: 52 calories, 1 g protein, .9 g carbohydrates, 5 g total fat, 10 mg cholesterol, 67 mg sodium

---

Pictured on page 6
PESTO CHEESE SPREAD

Preparation time: About 5 minutes
Cooking time: About 6 minutes

With purchased pesto sauce, you can whip up this tasty cheese spread in minutes. Serve with thick breadsticks and sliced vegetables.

- ⅓ cup pine nuts or slivered almonds
- 8 ounces ricotta cheese, at room temperature
- 8 ounces Neufchâtel cheese or mascarpone, at room temperature
- ⅓ cup pesto, purchased or homemade
  Salt
  Basil sprigs (optional)

Spread pine nuts in a shallow baking pan. Bake in a 350° oven until golden (about 6 minutes). Let cool briefly.

Meanwhile, beat ricotta, Neufchâtel, and pesto until well blended; season to taste with salt. Stir in half the nuts and mound in a bowl. If made ahead, cover and refrigerate until next day; store remaining nuts at room temperature.

Sprinkle with remaining pine nuts and garnish with basil, if desired. Serve at room temperature. Makes about 2 cups.

Per tablespoon: 45 calories, 2 g protein, 1 g carbohydrates, 4 g total fat, 8 mg cholesterol, 48 mg sodium

---

Pictured on page 19
STUFFED CAMEMBERT

Preparation time: About 15 minutes
Chilling time: At least 1 day

Camembert becomes the holder for a singular spread made with four different cheeses. Serve with a variety of your favorite crackers.

- 1 whole medium-ripe Camembert cheese (about 8 oz.), chilled
- 1 wedge (1¼ oz.) blue-veined cheese, crumbled, at room temperature
- 1 cup (4 oz.) shredded Cheddar cheese, at room temperature
- 1 small package (3 oz.) cream cheese, at room temperature
- 1 small clove garlic, minced or pressed
- 1 teaspoon *each* fresh basil and fresh oregano leaves or ½ teaspoon *each* dry basil and dry oregano leaves
- 1 tablespoon chopped parsley
- 2 tablespoons butter or margarine, at room temperature
- ¼ cup thinly sliced green onions (including tops)

With a sharp knife, cut around top of Camembert, about ¼ inch in from edge, cutting down about ½ inch into cheese. With a spoon, carefully scoop out cheese (including top rind), leaving a ¼-inch-thick shell. Wrap shell and refrigerate.

Place blue-veined cheese, Cheddar, cream cheese, and removed Camembert in a large bowl; then beat until smooth and creamy. Beat in garlic, basil, oregano, parsley, and butter; stir in onions. Mound cheese mixture in Camembert shell. Cover and refrigerate for at least a day or up to 4 days.

Serve at room temperature. Makes about 8 servings.

Per serving: 223 calories, 11 g protein, 1 g carbohydrates, 19 g total fat, 59 mg cholesterol, 468 mg sodium

CHÈVRE WITH MINT & CUMIN

◆

Preparation time: About 5 minutes

Add a special touch to purchased cheese by drizzling it with extra-virgin olive oil. Serve with toasted baguette slices.

- 1 log- or cake-shaped unripened goat cheese (12 oz.), such as Bûcheron
- 3 tablespoons extra-virgin olive oil
- ½ teaspoon cumin seeds, crushed
- 2 tablespoons chopped fresh mint leaves
- ¼ teaspoon ground red pepper (cayenne) or to taste

Place cheese on a small plate. Drizzle with oil. Sprinkle with cumin, mint, and pepper. Makes about 6 servings.

Per serving: 267 calories, 11 g protein, 4 g carbohydrates, 23 g total fat, 52 mg cholesterol, 350 mg sodium

Pictured on page 51
PEPPERED CHÈVRE WITH PEARS

◆

Preparation time: About 10 minutes

Roll fresh goat cheese in a savory blend of peppercorns, coriander, and lemon peel. Then spread the tangy coated log on pear slices.

- ½ teaspoon *each* black peppercorns, white peppercorns, and coriander seeds
- ½ teaspoon minced lemon peel (yellow part only)
- ½ teaspoon fresh lemon thyme leaves (optional)
- 1 log- or cake-shaped unripened goat cheese (4 oz.), such as Bûcheron
- 2 small firm-ripe Bartlett pears Lemon juice
  Lemon thyme sprigs (optional)
  Lemon wedges (optional)

In a spice grinder or blender, whirl black and white peppercorns, coriander, lemon peel, and, if desired, thyme leaves until seasonings form a coarse powder.

Transfer to wax paper. Roll cheese in mixture, pressing in seasonings on all sides. Core pears, cut each into 8 wedges, and sprinkle lightly with lemon juice.

Place cheese on a plate; garnish with thyme sprigs, if desired. Arrange pears and, if desired, lemon wedges beside cheese. Spread cheese on pear wedges. Makes 16 appetizers.

Per appetizer: 36 calories, 1 g protein, 3 g carbohydrates, 2 g total fat, 7 mg cholesterol, 44 mg sodium

NUT-STUDDED GARLIC-HERB CHEESE

◆

Preparation time: About 10 minutes
Chilling time: At least 2 hours
Cooking time: About 8 minutes

You can make your own herb spread by adding savory and garlic to cream cheese. For extra appeal, shape the mixture into a ball and cover with almonds.

- 1 large package (8 oz.) cream cheese, at room temperature
- 3 tablespoons lemon juice
- 1 teaspoon dry winter or summer savory
- ¼ to ½ teaspoon freshly ground pepper
- 1 clove garlic, minced or pressed
- ½ cup slivered almonds

Beat cream cheese until smooth. Beat in lemon juice, savory, pepper, and garlic. Shape mixture into a ball, wrap in wax paper or plastic wrap, and refrigerate for at least 2 hours or up to 2 days.

Shortly before serving, spread almonds in a shallow pan. Bake in a 350° oven until golden (about 8 minutes); let cool. Stud top and sides of cheese with almonds. Serve at room temperature. Makes about 1¼ cups.

Per tablespoon: 60 calories, 2 g protein, 1 g carbohydrates, 6 g total fat, 12 mg cholesterol, 34 mg sodium

GORGONZOLA CHEESE TORTA

◆

Preparation time: About 20 minutes
Chilling time: At least 1 hour

Butter-enriched cream cheese tempers the robust strength of Gorgonzola in this multitiered mold. Serve the simple spread with crisp crackers and sliced pears.

- 1 large package (8 oz.) cream cheese, at room temperature
- 1 cup (½ lb.) unsalted butter, at room temperature
- 12 ounces Gorgonzola or other blue-veined cheese, finely crumbled

Beat cream cheese and butter until very smoothly blended; set aside.

Cut two 18-inch squares of cheesecloth (or an 18-inch square of unbleached muslin); moisten with water, wring dry, and lay each out flat, one on top of the other. Use cloth to smoothly line a 4- to 5-cup straight-sided plain mold, such as a charlotte mold, loaf pan, or terrine; drape excess cloth over rim of mold.

Spread a third of the Gorgonzola in an even layer in mold. Top with a third of the cream cheese mixture, spreading evenly. Repeat layers, using all ingredients. Fold cloth over top and press down lightly to compact. Refrigerate for at least 1 hour or up to 5 days.

Grasp ends of cloth and lift torta from mold. Invert onto a plate and gently pull off cloth. Makes 16 servings.

Per serving: 226 calories, 6 g protein, .9 g carbohydrates, 23 g total fat, 63 mg cholesterol, 340 mg sodium

Easy on the host, Dried Tomato Torta (recipe on facing page) can be made well in advance of the party. Serve the creamy cheese spread on Pita Crisps (recipe on page 16) or crunchy baguette slices.

DRIED TOMATO TORTA

Pictured on facing page

Preparation time: About 20 minutes
Chilling time: About 20 minutes

Sun-dried tomatoes explain the bold color and unique flavor of this rich cheese spread. Serve on Garlic Toast (recipe on page 16) or toasted pita triangles and top with reserved tomato strips and basil leaves.

- 1 large package (8 oz.) cream cheese, at room temperature
- 1 cup (½ lb.) unsalted butter, at room temperature
- 1 cup (about 4 oz.) freshly grated Parmesan cheese
- ½ cup dried tomatoes packed in oil, drained (reserve oil)
  About 2 cups lightly packed basil leaves

Beat cream cheese, butter, and Parmesan cheese until very smoothly blended.

Cut 4 of the tomatoes into thin strips; set aside. In a blender or food processor, whirl remaining tomatoes, 2 tablespoons of the reserved oil from tomatoes, and about ½ cup of the cheese mixture until very smoothly puréed. Add purée mixture to cheese mixture and beat until blended. Cover and refrigerate until firm enough to shape (about 20 minutes).

Mound cheese on a platter. If made ahead, cover and refrigerate for up to 3 days.

Arrange basil and reserved tomato strips around torta. Makes 16 servings.

Per serving: 225 calories, 4 g protein, 3 g carbohydrates, 22 g total fat, 51 mg cholesterol, 320 mg sodium

BLACK CAVIAR PIE

Preparation time: About 25 minutes
Chilling time: At least 2 hours

A mustardy egg salad forms the crust of this creamy rich pie; black caviar tops the multilayered offering. Put thin slices of the pie on crackers or dark pumpernickel bread.

- 1 jar (3 to 4 oz.) black lumpfish or whitefish caviar
  Mustard Eggs (recipe follows)
- 1 cup chopped green onions (including tops)
- 1 jar (2 oz.) sliced pimentos, drained
- 1 large package (8 oz.) cream cheese, at room temperature
- ⅔ cup sour cream
  Dill sprigs
  Thin lemon slices

Empty caviar into a fine wire strainer and rinse with cold water; let drain. Cover and refrigerate. Meanwhile, prepare Mustard Eggs and spread in a 9-inch tart pan with a removable bottom. Sprinkle with onions and pimentos. Cover and refrigerate for 1 hour.

Mix cream cheese and sour cream until blended. Spoon about two-thirds of the mixture into pan. Using a pastry tube with a star tip, pipe remaining cream cheese mixture decoratively around edge. Cover and refrigerate for at least 1 hour or until next day.

Just before serving, remove sides of pan and spoon caviar into center of pie. Decorate with dill sprigs and lemon slices. Makes 16 servings.

Mustard Eggs. In a blender or food processor, whirl 6 **hard-cooked eggs;** ⅓ cup **butter** or margarine, at room temperature; 2 teaspoons *each* **Dijon mustard** and **white wine vinegar;** and 1 tablespoon chopped **fresh dill** or 1 teaspoon dill weed until smooth. Season to taste with **salt.**

Per serving: 151 calories, 5 g protein, 2 g carbohydrates, 14 g total fat, 146 mg cholesterol, 222 mg sodium

QUICK CHICKEN LIVER PÂTÉ

Preparation time: About 8 minutes
Cooking time: About 10 minutes
Chilling time: At least 3 hours

Present this smooth, thyme-accented spread in an attractive terrine or crock with thin slices of French bread alongside.

- 1 cup (½ lb.) plus 2 teaspoons butter or margarine, at room temperature
- 3 green onions (including tops), thinly sliced
- 1 pound chicken livers
- ½ cup dry red wine
- ¼ teaspoon salt
- ⅛ teaspoon *each* dry thyme leaves and pepper
- 2 tablespoons chopped parsley

In a wide frying pan, melt the 2 teaspoons butter over medium-high heat. Add onions and cook, stirring, until soft (about 3 minutes). Add chicken livers; cook, turning, until browned (about 3 more minutes). Stir in wine, salt, thyme, and pepper; reduce heat and simmer for 3 minutes. Stir in parsley.

Transfer mixture to a blender or food processor and whirl until smooth. Dice remaining 1 cup butter; with motor running, drop into blender, a few pieces at a time, and whirl until well combined. Cover and refrigerate for at least 3 hours or up to 4 days. Makes about 3 cups.

Per tablespoon: 48 calories, 2 g protein, .4 g carbohydrates, 4 g total fat, 52 mg cholesterol, 60 mg sodium

When the urge for a quick nibble strikes, you'll be glad to have these irresistible morsels on hand in the kitchen. All can be prepared in advance and stored from one day to two weeks before serving.

Whether you try seasoned nuts, candied popcorn, or crispy chips, you'll find these tempting edibles effortless to make. The hardest part is keeping enough of them around.

SWEET & SPICY ALMOND BRITTLE

Preparation time: About 5 minutes
Cooking time: About 10 minutes

This sugar-glazed almond confection boasts a Southwestern accent: it's sparked with chili powder and ground red pepper.

- 1　tablespoon chili powder
- ½　teaspoon *each* salt and ground red pepper (cayenne)
- 3　tablespoons salad oil
- ½　cup sugar
- 2　cups blanched almonds

Combine chili powder, salt, and pepper. Set aside.

Heat oil in a wide frying pan over medium-high heat. Add sugar and cook, stirring, until sugar is melted and begins to turn golden (about 4 minutes). Add almonds and cook, stirring, until sugar is a rich caramel color (about 4 more minutes). Add chili powder mixture and cook, stirring, for 1 more minute; be careful not to scorch nuts.

Immediately pour almonds onto a large sheet of foil, spreading so nuts are in a single layer. Let harden. Break into small pieces. Store airtight for up to 2 weeks. Makes 4 cups.

Per ¼ cup: 155 calories, 4 g protein, 10 g carbohydrates, 12 g total fat, 0 mg cholesterol, 75 mg sodium

MAKE-AHEAD MUNCHIES

SWEET SPICED PISTACHIOS

Preparation time: About 5 minutes
Cooking time: About 10 minutes

Although delicious alone, pistachios become crisp sweets when glazed with melted sugar and spices.

- 1　cup shelled salted pistachios
- ¼　cup sugar
- ½　teaspoon ground cinnamon
- ½　teaspoon ground mace or ground nutmeg

In a wide frying pan, toast pistachios over medium heat, shaking pan often, until golden (about 5 minutes). Sprinkle with sugar, cinnamon, and mace. Cook, stirring, until sugar is melted and nuts are glossy (about 5 more minutes). Pour onto a sheet of foil and let cool. Break nuts apart. Store airtight for up to a week. Makes about 1½ cups.

Per ¼ cup: 156 calories, 4 g protein, 14 g carbohydrates, 10 g total fat, 0 mg cholesterol, 2 mg sodium

CANDIED WALNUTS

Preparation time: About 10 minutes
Cooking time: About 8 minutes

Sugar and soy sauce coat walnut halves with a dark, crunchy covering. You can make this Chinese treat in a wok or frying pan.

- 2　cups (about 7 oz.) walnut halves
- 1　tablespoon soy sauce
- ¼　cup *each* granulated sugar and powdered sugar
　　Salad oil

In a 3- to 4-quart pan, cook walnuts in 2 quarts boiling water for 3 minutes. Drain well. Return to pan and mix with soy. Then stir in granulated and powdered sugars.

In a wok or wide frying pan, heat about 1½ inches oil to 275°F on a deep-frying thermometer. Add nut mixture and cook, stirring often, until nuts are deep golden brown (about 5 minutes). Lift out with a slotted spoon and place on a chilled 10- by 15-inch baking pan. Using oiled chopsticks or forks, immediately separate nuts. Let cool. Blot off excess oil with paper towels. Break nuts apart, if necessary.

Immediately store airtight for up to a week. Makes 2 cups.

Per ¼ cup: 229 calories, 4 g protein, 15 g carbohydrates, 19 g total fat, 0 mg cholesterol, 131 mg sodium

SPICED PECANS

Preparation time: About 5 minutes
Cooking time: About 3 minutes

Pecans, a favorite in the South, benefit from spicy Southern seasonings. The result will be enjoyed anywhere.

- ½　teaspoon *each* salt, paprika, and ground red pepper (cayenne)
- 1　teaspoon ground white pepper
- 1　tablespoon fresh or dry rosemary
- 2　tablespoons butter or margarine
- 1　tablespoon olive oil
- 10　ounces (about 2½ cups) pecan halves
- 1　tablespoon Worcestershire
- ½　teaspoon liquid hot pepper seasoning

Combine salt, paprika, red pepper, white pepper, and rosemary. Set aside.

Heat butter and oil in a wide frying pan over medium-high heat. When butter is melted, add pecans and cook, stirring, until slightly darker in color (about 1 minute). Add Worcestershire, hot pepper seasoning, and salt mixture. Continue cooking, stirring, until pecans are well browned (about 1½ more minutes); be careful not to scorch nuts. Let cool. Store airtight for up to 2 days. Makes 2½ cups.

Per ¼ cup: 225 calories, 2 g protein, 6 g carbohydrates, 23 g total fat, 6 mg cholesterol, 156 mg sodium

CURRIED RAISINS, PEANUTS & BANANA CHIPS

**Preparation time: About 5 minutes
Cooking time: About 2 minutes**

This spicy dried fruit and nut combination blends curried raisins and banana chips with peanuts. Dust the lively party mix with nutmeg.

¼ **cup salad oil**
1½ **teaspoons curry powder**
1 **cup raisins**
1 **cup *each* salted dry-roasted peanuts and dry banana chips
   Ground nutmeg**

Heat oil in a wide frying pan over medium-high heat. Add curry and cook, stirring, just until curry darkens slightly (about 30 seconds). Add raisins and cook, stirring, until puffed (about 1 more minute). Add peanuts and banana chips and cook, stirring, until coated. Pour onto paper towels. Blot gently with more

paper towels and sprinkle with nutmeg. Store airtight until next day. Makes 3 cups.

Per ¼ cup: 174 calories, 4 g protein, 20 g carbohydrates, 11 g total fat, 0 mg cholesterol, 108 mg sodium

SWEET POTATO CHIPS

**Preparation time: About 15 minutes
Cooking time: About 20 minutes**

Here's a crunchy, distinctly sweeter alternative to regular potato chips. Be sure to cut the potatoes into uniform-size slices and cook in small batches.

2 **large (about 2 lbs. *total*) sweet potatoes or yams, peeled
   Salad oil
   Salt**

Rinse potatoes and pat dry. To cut slices about ¹⁄₁₆ inch thick, use a food slicer with an adjustable blade; push or hold potatoes crosswise to blade to cut rounds. For thicker, ⅛-inch slices, adjust blade on a manually operated slicer to this dimension or use slicing blade (about 3mm size) of a food processor and apply pressure lightly but evenly while cutting. Pat dry.

In a deep 3- to 4-quart pan, heat about 1½ inches oil to 300°F on a deep-frying thermometer. With a slotted spoon, lower potatoes, a spoonful at a time, into oil (do not crowd). Cook, turning about every 2 minutes, until chips are lightly browned (about 3 minutes for thin slices, longer for thicker ones). Lift out with a slotted spoon and drain on paper towels.

Season to taste with salt. Store airtight for up to 5 days. Makes about 3 quarts.

Per ¼ cup: 29 calories, .2 g protein, 3 g carbohydrates, 2 g total fat, 0 mg cholesterol, 2 mg sodium

BAKED CANDIED POPCORN

**Preparation time: About 5 minutes
Cooking time: About 20 minutes**

Peanuts lend added crunch to this favorite popcorn treat.

¼ **cup salad oil**
1 **cup popcorn kernels**
1½ **cups salted or unsalted dry-roasted peanuts**
½ **cup (¼ lb.) butter or margarine**
½ **cup light or dark molasses**
½ **cup honey**

Heat oil in a 5- to 6-quart pan over medium-high heat. Add popcorn kernels, cover, and cook, shaking pan occasionally, until kernels have nearly stopped popping (about 6 minutes). Pour into a large bowl; discard any unpopped kernels. Stir in peanuts.

In same pan, melt butter over low heat. Add molasses and honey, increase heat to high, and cook, stirring, until bubbles begin to form (about 5 minutes); immediately pour over popped corn mixture, stirring to coat evenly.

Spread into two 10- by 15-inch baking pans. Bake in a 350° oven, stirring often, until coating is slightly darker (about 8 minutes, longer if margarine is used); switch pan positions halfway through cooking. Let cool. Store airtight for up to 3 days. Makes 6 quarts.

Per ¼ cup: 44 calories, .8 g protein, 5 g carbohydrates, 3 g total fat, 3 mg cholesterol, 30 mg sodium

Pictured on facing page

CREAMY BRAUNSCHWEIGER APPETIZER

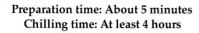

Preparation time: About 5 minutes
Chilling time: At least 4 hours

Spread this simplified pâté-like appetizer on pumpernickel or cocktail-size rye rounds.

½ **pound braunschweiger or other liver sausage, casing removed**
1 **cup sour cream**
1 **teaspoon Worcestershire**
6 **green onions (including tops), chopped**
  About ⅓ cup chopped parsley
3 **drops liquid hot pepper seasoning**
2 **to 3 tablespoons prepared horseradish**

Cut sausage into chunks. In a blender or food processor, whirl sausage, sour cream, Worcestershire, onions, ⅓ cup of the parsley, hot pepper seasoning, and horseradish until smooth and creamy. Transfer to a bowl. Cover and refrigerate for at least 4 hours or up to 2 days.

Garnish with additional parsley, if desired. Makes 2½ cups.

Per tablespoon: 34 calories, 1 g protein, .7 g carbohydrates, 3 g total fat, 11 mg cholesterol, 71 mg sodium

Pictured on facing page

QUICK TUNA-ANCHOVY SPREAD

Preparation time: About 5 minutes
Marinating time: At least 20 minutes

By taking advantage of bottled dressing and other ingredients easily kept on hand, you can have this zesty spread ready to serve in less than half an hour.

1 **can (7 oz.) chunk-style tuna, drained**
1 **can (2 oz.) anchovy fillets, drained**
⅛ **teaspoon *each* dry mustard and dry oregano leaves**
  Dash of ground red pepper (cayenne)
1 **tablespoon pickle relish**
1 **teaspoon lemon juice**
¼ **cup bottled French dressing**
  Lemon slice (optional)
  Chopped parsley (optional)

Break tuna into bite-size pieces. Coarsely chop anchovies and add to tuna with mustard, oregano, pepper, pickle relish, lemon juice, and French dressing. Toss lightly. Transfer to a dish. Cover and refrigerate for at least 20 minutes or until next day.

Garnish with lemon and sprinkle with parsley, if desired. Makes about 2¼ cups.

Per tablespoon: 36 calories, 3 g protein, .8 g carbohydrates, 2 g total fat, 3 mg cholesterol, 161 mg sodium

POTTED SHRIMP WITH CHERVIL

Preparation time: About 25 minutes
Chilling time: At least 2 hours

A favorite for afternoon tea in England, this delicate shrimp butter is a perfect appetizer anytime. Try serving it with buttery crackers or toasted baguette slices.

¾ **pound small cooked shrimp**
½ **cup (¼ lb.) butter or margarine, at room temperature**
1½ **tablespoons lime or lemon juice**
¼ **teaspoon salt**
⅛ **teaspoon ground white pepper**
¼ **cup lightly packed fresh chervil**

In a blender or food processor, whirl shrimp, butter, lime juice, salt, and pepper until mixture is well combined. Add chervil and whirl until blended. Cover and refrigerate for at least 2 hours or until next day. Serve at room temperature. Makes about 2 cups.

Per tablespoon: 36 calories, 2 g protein, .1 g carbohydrates, 3 g total fat, 29 mg cholesterol, 70 mg sodium

Pictured on facing page

DILLED SHRIMP MOUSSE

Preparation time: About 15 minutes
Cooking time: About 2 minutes
Chilling time: At least 4 hours

Use your favorite mold to showcase this creamy pink concoction. The dill-accented shrimp spread is delicious on thin slices of whole-grain bread.

¾ **cup tomato juice**
1 **envelope unflavored gelatin**
1 **cup sour cream**
¼ **teaspoon Worcestershire**
1 **tablespoon lemon juice**
1½ **teaspoons dill weed**
½ **pound small cooked shrimp**
16 **butter lettuce leaves, washed and crisped**
  Dill sprigs (optional)
1 **cinnamon stick (½ in. long), optional**

Pour tomato juice into a 1- to 1½-quart pan; sprinkle with gelatin and let stand for 5 minutes to soften. Place pan over low heat and cook, stirring, until gelatin is dissolved. Remove from heat and let cool.

In a bowl, beat gelatin mixture, sour cream, Worcestershire, lemon juice, and dill weed until well blended. Chop half the shrimp and add to sour cream mixture. Pour into a 2½- to 3-cup mold. Cover and refrigerate for at least 4 hours or until next day.

Unmold onto a plate. Arrange lettuce and remaining shrimp around mousse. Garnish with dill sprigs and cinnamon stick, if desired. Makes 2½ cups.

Per tablespoon: 66 calories, 5 g protein, 2 g carbohydrates, 4 g total fat, 45 mg cholesterol, 110 mg sodium

Holiday parties are easy to orchestrate when you offer a medley of simple-to-prepare spreads: Creamy Braun-schweiger Appetizer (recipe on facing page), Dilled Shrimp Mousse (recipe on facing page), Sweet & Sour Onion Spread (recipe on page 29), and Quick Tuna-Anchovy Spread (recipe on facing page).

TURKEY RILLETTES

Preparation time: About 30 minutes
Cooking time: About 4 hours

The French make rillettes (pro-nounced ree-YET) with pork, duck, or goose and an abundance of fat. This leaner version is made with turkey thigh meat instead. Thick slices of French bread are the perfect accompaniment.

- 3 to 3½ pounds turkey thighs
- ½ teaspoon *each* pepper and dry thyme leaves
- ¼ teaspoon *each* dry sage leaves and dry marjoram leaves
- 1 clove garlic, minced or pressed
- ¼ cup finely chopped shallots
- ⅔ cup dry white wine
- ¼ cup unsalted butter or margarine, at room temperature
   Salt

Place turkey in a 4- to 5-quart pan and add pepper, thyme, sage, marjoram, garlic, and shallots; pour in wine. Cover and bake in a 250° oven until meat falls apart when prodded with a fork (about 4 hours).

Drain and reserve juices, refrigerate until cool, and then skim and discard fat. Meanwhile, discard skin and bones from turkey and shred meat; then chop.

Mix meat, juices, and butter until well blended. Season to taste with salt. Spoon mixture into a 5½- to 6½-cup terrine or crock.

If made ahead, cover and refrigerate for up to 3 days. Serve at room temperature. Makes about 5½ cups.

Per tablespoon: 14 calories, 1 g protein, .1 g carbohydrates, .8 g total fat, 7 mg cholesterol, 6 mg sodium

---

Pictured on page 6
BAKED VEGETABLES PROVENÇAL

Preparation time: About 20 minutes
Cooking time: About 50 minutes

Eggplant, bell pepper, and onion are baked in olive oil and tossed with fresh tomatoes, parsley, and wine vinegar for a hearty vegetable mixture you can spread on Garlic Toast (recipe on page 16) or other toasted bread slices.

- 4 tablespoons olive oil
- 1 large eggplant (about 1½ lbs.), ends trimmed, cut in half lengthwise
- 1 large red bell pepper, cut in half, stemmed, and seeded
- 1 medium-size onion, cut in half
- 2 large pear-shaped tomatoes, coarsely chopped
- 2 tablespoons white wine vinegar
- ¼ cup chopped Italian parsley
   Salt and pepper
   Niçoise olives (optional)
   Italian parsley sprigs (optional)

Pour 2 tablespoons of the oil into a 10- by 15-inch baking pan. Lay eggplant, bell pepper, and onion, cut sides down, in oil. Bake in a 350° oven until eggplant is very soft when pressed (about 50 minutes). Let cool briefly.

Trim off and discard skin from eggplant. Coarsely chop eggplant, bell pepper, and onion. Place in a strainer along with tomatoes; gently press out excess liquid. Transfer to a bowl. Stir in vinegar, chopped parsley, and remaining 2 tablespoons oil. Season to taste with salt and pepper.

If made ahead, cover and refrigerate until next day. Serve at room temperature, stirring before serving.

Garnish with olives and parsley sprigs, if desired. Makes about 4 cups.

Per tablespoon: 11 calories, .1 g protein, .9 g carbohydrates, .8 g total fat, 0 mg cholesterol, .8 mg sodium

---

FRESH MUSHROOM PÂTÉ

Preparation time: About 15 minutes
Cooking time: About 15 minutes

This creamy spread works equally well on crackers, toast rounds, or crisp raw vegetables. Use fresh mushrooms: mild-flavored regular (button shaped), meaty shiitake, or a combination of both. Or experiment with another variety of your choice.

- ¼ cup butter or margarine
- ⅓ pound fresh mushrooms, such as regular, shiitake, or a combination, coarsely chopped
- ⅓ cup finely chopped onion
- 1 tablespoon dry sherry or regular-strength chicken broth
- 1 small package (3 oz.) cream cheese, at room temperature
- ¼ cup minced parsley

In a wide frying pan, melt butter over medium heat. Add mushrooms and onion and cook, stirring often, until mushrooms are browned (about 15 minutes). Mix in sherry.

In a bowl, beat cream cheese and parsley until blended. Stir in mushroom mixture.

If made ahead, cover and refrigerate for up to 3 days. Serve at room temperature. Makes 1 cup.

Per tablespoon: 49 calories, .7 g protein, 1 g carbohydrates, 5 g total fat, 14 mg cholesterol, 47 mg sodium

OLIVE PURÉE

Preparation time: About 5 minutes

With olives, anchovies, and capers in the cupboard, you can assemble this robust treat in minutes. Spread it on baguette slices and top with slivers of sun-dried tomatoes, if you like.

- 1 **can (2¼ oz.) black ripe olives, drained**
- ¼ **cup drained capers**
- 2 **teaspoons Dijon mustard**
- 5 **drained canned anchovy fillets**
- ¼ **teaspoon *each* cracked bay leaves and dry thyme leaves**
- 1 **large clove garlic**
- 1 **tablespoon olive or salad oil**

In a blender or food processor, whirl olives, capers, mustard, anchovies, bay, thyme, garlic, and oil until smoothly puréed. Serve at room temperature. Makes ½ cup.

Per tablespoon: 37 calories, .8 g protein, .6 g carbohydrates, 4 g total fat, 1 mg cholesterol, 299 mg sodium

Pictured on page 27
SWEET & SOUR ONION SPREAD

Preparation time: About 10 minutes
Cooking time: About 30 minutes

The slowly cooked sweet onions that go into this spread can be prepared a day in advance and then mixed with yogurt just before serving. Put out toasted pumpernickel bread for this lean, tangy-sweet appetizer.

- 2 **tablespoons salad oil**
- 3 **large onions, thinly sliced**
- 1 **cup plain yogurt**
- 1 **tablespoon rice vinegar or cider vinegar**
  Salt
  Coarsely ground pepper
  Cherry tomato halves (optional)
  Parsley sprigs (optional)

Heat oil in a wide frying pan over medium heat. Add onions and cook, stirring occasionally, until very soft (about 30 minutes). Let cool. (At this point, you may cover and refrigerate until next day; bring to room temperature before continuing.)

Mix onions, yogurt, and vinegar. Season to taste with salt. Spoon into a bowl and sprinkle with pepper. Garnish with tomato and parsley, if desired. Makes 2 cups.

Per tablespoon: 17 calories, .5 g protein, 2 g carbohydrates, 1 g total fat, .4 mg cholesterol, 5 mg sodium

ONION-CHEESE SPREAD

Preparation time: About 15 minutes
Cooking time: About 30 minutes

The sweet flavor of slowly cooked onions combines winningly with tangy goat cheese and prosciutto. Serve the warm spread on toasted cocktail-size rye bread.

- 2 **tablespoons butter or margarine**
- 3 **large onions, thinly sliced**
- 1 **teaspoon fresh thyme leaves or ½ teaspoon dry thyme leaves**
- 2 **ounces thinly sliced prosciutto, slivered**
- ¼ **pound mild goat cheese, such as Montrachet or Bûcheron, crumbled**

In a wide frying pan, melt butter over medium heat. Add onions and thyme and cook, stirring occasionally, until onions are very soft (about 30 minutes).

Add prosciutto and cheese and cook, stirring, until cheese is melted. Makes about 1 cup.

Per tablespoon: 55 calories, 2 g protein, 3 g carbohydrates, 4 g total fat, 12 mg cholesterol, 106 mg sodium

GINGER & MUSTARD SEED CHUTNEY

Preparation time: About 15 minutes
Cooking time: About 25 minutes

This bold tomato relish blends many seasonings into a sweet-sour, spicy balance. You can store the chutney in the refrigerator for up to three weeks. Spoon it over cream cheese and spread on crackers.

- 3 **tablespoons salad oil**
- 3 **tablespoons mustard seeds**
- 1 **medium-size onion, finely chopped**
- 1 **cup *each* firmly packed brown sugar and red wine vinegar**
- 3 **medium-size tomatoes, cored, peeled, and chopped**
- 2 **tablespoons *each* minced fresh ginger and dark molasses**
- 4 **large cloves garlic, minced or pressed**
- 1 **stick cinnamon (2½ to 3 in. long)**
- ½ **teaspoon salt**
- ¼ **teaspoon whole cloves**
- ¼ **teaspoon ground red pepper (cayenne) or crushed dried hot red chiles**
- ¼ **cup finely chopped cilantro (coriander)**

Heat oil in a 2- to 3-quart pan over medium-high heat. Add mustard seeds and cook, stirring often, until seeds begin to pop. Add onion and continue cooking, stirring, until soft (about 5 minutes).

Add sugar, vinegar, tomatoes, ginger, molasses, garlic, cinnamon, salt, cloves, and pepper. Boil gently, stirring occasionally, until mixture is reduced to 3 cups (about 10 minutes). Add cilantro and continue cooking, stirring occasionally, for 5 more minutes. Serve warm or at room temperature.

If made ahead, cool, cover, and refrigerate for up to 3 weeks. Makes about 3 cups.

Per tablespoon: 33 calories, .3 g protein, 6 g carbohydrates, 1 g total fat, 0 mg cholesterol, 26 mg sodium

Warm up your next party with our hot hors d'oeuvres. Start with sausage- and spinach-stuffed Florentine Mushrooms (recipe on page 65), Baked Shrimp with Garlic (recipe on page 61), and Summer Squash Squares (recipe on page 32).

30

HOT
MORSELS

Sweet or savory, the aroma of food cooking is an irresistible invitation to dine. Meat grilled to juicy perfection, stuffed vegetables hot from the steamer, and pastries browned in the oven greet guests warmly.

Happily for the cook, just because an appetizer is served hot (or allowed to cool just to room temperature) doesn't mean that it has to be fully prepared at the very last minute: meat can be marinated, vegetables filled, and dough formed all in advance. Still, it's the final introduction of heat that lends the welcome finishing touch.

SUPER NACHOS

◆

Preparation time: About 30 minutes
Cooking time: About 30 minutes

This layered casserole of refried beans, meat, chiles, and cheese feeds a crowd. Tuck tortilla chips around the dish for an attractive presentation and easy eating.

½ pound *each* lean ground beef and chorizo sausage, casing removed; or 1 pound lean ground beef
1 large onion, chopped
Salt
Liquid hot pepper seasoning
1 or 2 cans (about 1 lb. *each*) refried beans
1 can (4 oz.) whole green chiles (for mildest flavor, remove seeds and pith), chopped
2 to 3 cups (8 to 12 oz.) shredded jack or mild Cheddar cheese
¾ cup prepared green or red taco sauce
Fried Tortilla Chips (recipe on page 16) or packaged tortilla chips
Garnishes (suggestions follow)

Crumble ground beef and sausage into a wide frying pan over medium heat. Add onion and cook, stirring, until meat is no longer pink (about 7 minutes). Discard fat; season to taste with salt and hot pepper seasoning.

Spread beans on a large heatproof platter. Top evenly with meat mixture. Sprinkle evenly with chiles and cheese, and drizzle with taco sauce. (At this point, you may cover and refrigerate until next day.)

Bake in a 400° oven until hot (about 20 minutes). Meanwhile, prepare Fried Tortilla Chips and garnishes of your choice.

Quickly garnish platter, mounding Guacamole and sour cream, if used, in center. Tuck chips around edges. If desired, keep hot on an electric warming tray. Makes about 1 dozen servings.

Garnishes. Prepare some or all of the following: About ¼ cup chopped **green onions** (including some tops), about 1 cup pitted **ripe olives**, **Guacamole** (recipe on page 15), about 1 cup **sour cream**, **cilantro** (coriander) or parsley **sprigs.**

Per serving: 366 calories, 18 g protein, 26 g carbohydrates, 20 g total fat, 43 mg cholesterol, 659 mg sodium

SCOTCH BAKED EGGS

◆

Preparation time: About 15 minutes
Cooking time: About 30 minutes

Begin a Sunday brunch with this eye-catching sausage-and-egg combination. You can prepare the dish a day ahead and then bake it just before serving.

2½ pounds bulk pork sausage
8 hard-cooked eggs, chilled and shelled

Divide sausage into 8 equal portions. On wax paper, flatten each portion into a patty about ⅜ inch thick. With moistened hands, wrap an egg in each patty, smoothing surfaces until free of cracks. (At this point, you may cover and refrigerate until next day.)

Place sausage-wrapped eggs, slightly apart, in a shallow baking pan. Bake in upper third of a 450° oven until meat is no longer pink inside when cut (about 30 minutes). Drain briefly on paper towels. Cut in half crosswise. Makes 16 appetizers.

Per appetizer: 161 calories, 10 g protein, .6 g carbohydrates, 13 g total fat, 134 mg cholesterol, 467 mg sodium

Pictured on page 30
SUMMER SQUASH SQUARES

◆

Preparation time: About 30 minutes
Cooking time: About 40 minutes
Cooling time: At least 15 minutes

Choose your favorite summer squash variety for this easy-to-prepare custardy dish.

¼ cup salad oil
1 small onion, finely chopped
1 clove garlic, minced or pressed
2½ cups shredded summer squash, such as crookneck, zucchini, or pattypan
6 eggs, lightly beaten
⅓ cup fine dry bread crumbs
½ teaspoon *each* salt, dry basil leaves, and dry oregano leaves
¼ teaspoon pepper
3 cups (12 oz.) shredded Cheddar cheese
½ cup grated Parmesan cheese
¼ cup sesame seeds
Basil sprigs (optional)

Heat oil in a wide frying pan over medium-high heat. Add onion and cook, stirring, until soft (about 5 minutes). Add garlic and squash; cook, stirring, until squash is tender (about 3 more minutes). Set aside.

In a bowl, mix eggs, bread crumbs, salt, dry basil, oregano, pepper, and Cheddar; stir in squash mixture. Spread in a greased 9- by 13-inch baking dish. Sprinkle with Parmesan and sesame seeds. Bake in a 325° oven until set when touched in center (about 30 minutes). Let cool for at least 15 minutes.

Cut into 1-inch squares and arrange on a platter. Garnish with basil sprigs, if desired. Serve warm or at room temperature. Makes about 10 dozen appetizers.

Per appetizer: 24 calories, 1 g protein, .5 g carbohydrates, 2 g total fat, 14 mg cholesterol, 38 mg sodium

CHEESE-MUSHROOM FINGERS

◆

Preparation time: About 20 minutes
Cooking time: About 45 minutes
Cooling time: At least 15 minutes

Here's cheese custard for a crowd. Onion, bell pepper, and mushrooms bake along with jack and cottage cheese to a creamy consistency in these bite-size treats.

- ½ cup (¼ lb.) butter or margarine
- 1 pound mushrooms, sliced
- 1 large onion, chopped
- 2 cloves garlic, minced or pressed
- 1 large green bell pepper, seeded and chopped
- 10 eggs
- 2 cups small curd cottage cheese
- 4 cups (1 lb.) shredded jack cheese
- ½ cup all-purpose flour
- 1 teaspoon baking powder
- ¾ teaspoon *each* ground nutmeg, dry basil leaves, and salt

In a wide frying pan, melt butter over medium-high heat. Add mushrooms, onion, and garlic. Cook stirring, until onion is soft (about 7 minutes). Add bell pepper and cook, stirring, for 1 more minute; set aside.

In a large bowl, beat eggs, cottage cheese, jack, flour, baking powder, nutmeg, basil, and salt until blended; stir in mushroom mixture. Spread on a greased 10- by 15-inch rimmed baking sheet. Bake in a 350° oven until set when lightly touched in center (about 35 minutes). Let cool for at least 15 minutes.

Cut into ¾- by 2-inch fingers. Serve warm or at room temperature. Makes about 8 dozen appetizers.

Per appetizer: 43 calories, 3 g protein, 1 g carbohydrates, 3 g total fat, 29 mg cholesterol, 81 mg sodium

CRABBY JACK QUESADILLAS

◆

Preparation time: About 15 minutes
Cooking time: About 20 minutes

Flour tortillas with a crabmeat filling bake quickly into crisp quesadillas.

Chile-Cilantro Sauce (recipe follows)
- ¼ pound crabmeat
- 2 cups (8 oz.) shredded jack cheese
- 1 cup thinly sliced green onions (including tops)
- 10 flour tortillas (7- to 8-in. diameter)

Prepare Chile-Cilantro Sauce; keep warm.

In a bowl, lightly mix crabmeat, cheese, and onions. Place 5 of the tortillas in a single layer on two 14- by 17-inch baking sheets. Evenly spread each with crab mixture to within ¾ inch of edges. Top with remaining tortillas.

Bake in a 450° oven until cheese is melted and tortillas are lightly browned (about 7 minutes). Cut each into 6 wedges.

Offer with sauce for dipping. Makes 2½ dozen appetizers.

Per appetizer: 71 calories, 4 g protein, 8 g carbohydrates, 2 g total fat, 10 mg cholesterol, 121 mg sodium

Chile-Cilantro Sauce. Place 4 medium-size fresh **Anaheim chiles** on a baking sheet. Broil 2 inches below heat, turning often, until browned and blistered (about 5 minutes); let cool. Pull off and discard skin, stems, and seeds. Chop coarsely.

In a blender or food processor, whirl chiles, ¼ cup **dry white wine**, 1 tablespoon **lemon juice**, and 1 medium-size **shallot**, chopped, until smooth. Pour into a 2- to 3-quart pan and boil over high heat, stirring, until reduced to ⅓ cup (about 5 minutes).

Return mixture to blender. Add 1 cup firmly packed **cilantro** (coriander) and whirl until smooth, scraping container sides often. With motor running, slowly add ¼ cup hot melted **butter** or margarine, whirling until blended; scrape sides once or twice. Makes about 1 cup.

Per tablespoon: 29 calories, .2 g protein, .8 g carbohydrates, 3 g total fat, 8 mg cholesterol, 31 mg sodium

TOMATO-AVOCADO QUESADILLAS

◆

Preparation time: About 20 minutes
Cooking time: About 20 minutes

Tomatoes tame the heat of quesadillas filled with cheese, zucchini, chiles, and onion.

- 1⅔ cups Guacamole (recipe on page 15)
- 2 tablespoons salad oil
- 1 medium-size onion, finely chopped
- 2 teaspoons minced serrano or jalapeño chiles
- 1 cup finely chopped zucchini
- 8 whole wheat tortillas (9-in. diameter)
- 3 cups (12 oz.) shredded jack or mild Cheddar cheese
- 2 medium-size tomatoes, chopped

Prepare Guacamole; set aside.

Heat oil in a wide frying pan over medium heat. Add onion and chiles and cook, stirring, until onion is soft (about 7 minutes). Add zucchini and cook, stirring, until tender-crisp (about 4 more minutes).

Place 4 of the tortillas in a single layer on two 14- by 17-inch baking sheets. Evenly cover each with ¾ cup of the cheese and ¼ cup of the vegetable mixture. Top with remaining tortillas. Bake in a 450° oven until cheese is melted and tortillas are lightly browned (about 7 minutes). Cut each into 6 wedges. Top with tomatoes and Guacamole. Makes 2 dozen appetizers.

Per appetizer: 142 calories, 5 g protein, 11 g carbohydrates, 9 g total fat, 12 mg cholesterol, 205 mg sodium

Pictured on facing page

APPETIZER MINI-QUICHES

◆

Preparation time: About 1 hour
Cooking time: About 20 minutes

Ham and chiles flavor the custard in these bite-size quiches.

    Flaky Pastry (recipe follows)
    Ham & Green Chile Filling
    (recipe follows)
 2 **eggs**
 ¾ **cup sour cream**

Prepare Flaky Pastry. On a floured board, roll dough ¹⁄₁₆ inch thick. Cut into 2-inch circles, rerolling scraps to make about 72 circles. Fit into bottoms and partway up sides of 1¾-inch muffin cups.

    Prepare Ham & Green Chile Filling. Place a heaping teaspoon of the filling in each cup. Beat eggs lightly; beat in sour cream until smooth. Spoon about 1 teaspoon of the egg mixture into each cup.

    Bake in a 375° oven until tops are lightly browned (about 20 minutes). Let cool for 5 minutes; then tip quiches out of pans. Serve warm or at room temperature.

    If made ahead, let cool completely, wrap airtight, and refrigerate until next day; to reheat, spread quiches in a single layer in a shallow pan and place in a 350° oven until hot (about 10 minutes). Makes about 6 dozen appetizers.

Flaky Pastry. Mix 2 cups **all-purpose flour** and ½ teaspoon *each* **salt** and **chili powder**. Cut in ⅓ cup firm **butter** or margarine and ⅓ cup **solid vegetable shortening** until mixture resembles fine crumbs. Beat 1 **egg;** add enough cold **water** to make ¼ cup. Add to flour mixture, 1 tablespoon at a time, mixing until dough holds together. Shape into a ball.

Ham & Green Chile Filling. Mix ¾ cup finely diced cooked **ham** (about 3 oz.), 3 tablespoons chopped canned **green chiles,** ¼ cup chopped **green onions** (including tops), and 1½ cups (6 oz.) shredded **jack cheese.**

Per appetizer: 48 calories, 2 g protein, 3 g carbohydrates, 3 g total fat, 15 mg cholesterol, 60 mg sodium

NIPPY CHEESE PUFFS

◆

Preparation time: About 15 minutes
Cooking time: About 35 minutes

Here's a version of the classic French cheese puff, *gougère.*

 1 **cup water**
 ½ **cup (¼ lb.) butter or margarine**
 ⅛ **teaspoon ground nutmeg**
 1 **cup all-purpose flour**
 4 **eggs**
 1 **cup (4 oz.) lightly packed finely shredded sharp Cheddar or Asiago cheese**

In a 2- to 3-quart pan, stir water, butter, and nutmeg over medium-high heat until butter is melted. Add flour all at once, stirring until mixture leaves sides of pan and forms a ball (about 2 minutes). Remove from heat and transfer to a bowl; let cool briefly.

    Add eggs, one at a time, beating well after each addition. Stir in ½ cup of the cheese. Drop by spoonfuls about 1½ inches in diameter onto greased baking sheets, spacing puffs about 2 inches apart. Sprinkle with remaining ½ cup cheese.

    Bake in a 400° oven until golden brown (about 20 minutes). Turn off oven. Pierce each puff in several places. Return to oven until crisp (about 10 minutes). Makes about 3 dozen appetizers.

Per appetizer: 56 calories, 2 g protein, 3 g carbohydrates, 4 g total fat, 34 mg cholesterol, 53 mg sodium

ONION TARTS

◆

Preparation time: About 45 minutes
Cooking time: About 50 minutes

Pimentos and ripe olives peek out from the latticework of these Spanish pies. Known as *tortas de cebollas,* they're an elegant addition to a tapas party.

 ⅓ **cup olive or salad oil**
 3 **large onions, thinly sliced**
 ¼ **teaspoon ground nutmeg**
 ½ **teaspoon salt**
    Tart Shells (recipe follows)
 3 **eggs, lightly beaten**
 ¼ **cup sliced ripe olives**
 2 **to 3 tablespoons sliced pimentos**

Heat oil in a wide frying pan over medium heat. Add onions, nutmeg, and salt; cook, stirring occasionally, until onions are very soft (about 30 minutes). Let cool. Meanwhile, prepare Tart Shells.

    Combine onions and eggs; evenly pour mixture into shells. Trim dough about ½ inch above filling. On a floured board, roll out trimmings, cut into ¾-inch-wide strips, and weave over each tart to make a lattice topping. Fill spaces between lattices with olive and pimento slices. Bake in a 400° oven until pastry is golden (about 20 minutes); let cool briefly.

    Cut each pie into 12 wedges. Makes 2 dozen appetizers.

Tart Shells. Mix 1⅔ cups **all-purpose flour** and ¼ teaspoon **salt.** Cut in ½ cup (¼ lb.) firm **butter** or margarine until mixture resembles fine crumbs. Stirring with a fork, gradually add 2 tablespoons **salad oil;** then add 2 to 4 tablespoons cold **water,** 1 tablespoon at a time, mixing until dough holds together. Shape into 2 equal-size balls. On a floured board, roll each ball into a 12-inch circle. Fit into two 8-inch pie pans.

Per appetizer: 121 calories, 2 g protein, 8 g carbohydrates, 9 g total fat, 37 mg cholesterol, 126 mg sodium

*Guests will gobble up the golden goodies—Appetizer
Mini-Quiches (recipe on facing page)—in this basket.
They're perfect for a backyard barbecue or a more formal
dinner party.*

Pictured on page 83

SMOKED SALMON & HERBED CHEESE TARTS

Preparation time: About 45 minutes
Chilling time: At least 30 minutes
Cooking time: About 12 minutes

Puff pastry forms the base for an easy-to-prepare filling of smoked salmon and herbed garlic cream cheese.

1 **sheet (half a 17¼-oz. package) frozen puff pastry, thawed**
⅓ **cup (about 3 oz.) shredded or finely chopped smoked salmon or lox**
4 **ounces cream cheese flavored with herbs and garlic, at room temperature**
Marjoram or parsley sprigs (optional)

Unfold pastry sheet on a lightly floured board and roll into an 11-inch square. Cut into 2-inch circles, re-rolling scraps to make about 36. Fit into bottoms and partway up sides of 1¾-inch muffin cups.

In a small bowl, mix salmon and cream cheese. Place a scant teaspoon of the mixture in each cup. Cover and refrigerate for at least 30 minutes or up to 2 hours.

Bake, uncovered, in a 450° oven until golden brown (about 12 minutes). Let cool for 5 minutes; then tip tarts out of pans.

Garnish each tart with marjoram, if desired. Makes about 3 dozen appetizers.

Per appetizer: 42 calories, 1 g protein, 3 g carbohydrates, 3 g total fat, 3 mg cholesterol, 66 mg sodium

SCALLOP TARTS

Preparation time: About 20 minutes
Cooking time: About 25 minutes

Savory cheese pastry holds an elegant filling of sweet bay scallops.

Cheese Tart Shells (recipe follows)
⅓ **cup *each* dry white wine and whipping cream**
2 **teaspoons lemon juice**
1 **teaspoon Dijon mustard**
¼ **teaspoon dry tarragon leaves**
1 **small shallot, finely chopped**
½ **pound bay scallops, rinsed and dried**
2 **tablespoons grated Parmesan cheese**

Prepare Cheese Tart Shells; set aside.

In a wide frying pan, bring wine, cream, lemon juice, mustard, tarragon, and shallot to a boil over medium-high heat. Add scallops and cook, stirring often, until opaque when cut (about 2 minutes). Remove from heat. Lift scallops from pan, drain, and spoon into tart shells.

Boil liquid in pan over high heat until reduced by about half (about 5 minutes). Spoon over scallops and sprinkle with cheese. Arrange tarts on a baking sheet. Bake in a 400° oven until hot (about 5 minutes). Makes 15 appetizers.

Cheese Tart Shells. Mix ¾ cup **all-purpose flour,** ⅓ cup finely shredded **Swiss cheese,** and 2 tablespoons **grated Parmesan cheese.** Cut in ¼ cup cold **butter** or margarine until mixture resembles coarse crumbs. Gradually add ½ teaspoon **Worcestershire** and 1½ to 3 tablespoons cold **water,** mixing until dough holds together. Shape into a ball.

Divide into 15 portions. Press each into a shallow 1½- to 2-inch tart pan. Pierce in several places with a fork and arrange on a baking sheet. Bake in a 400° oven until golden brown (about 12 minutes). Let cool; then carefully remove shells.

Per appetizer: 95 calories, 5 g protein, 6 g carbohydrates, 6 g total fat, 22 mg cholesterol, 101 mg sodium

Pictured on page 83

SHRIMP & FETA FILA TRIANGLES

Preparation time: About 45 minutes
Cooking time: About 10 minutes

Delicate fila dough encases a creamy filling of feta cheese and tiny shrimp.

Shrimp & Feta Cheese Filling (recipe follows)
6 **sheets fila pastry (about ¼ of a 1-lb. package), thawed if frozen**
½ **cup (¼ lb.) butter or margarine, melted**

Prepare Shrimp & Feta Cheese Filling; set aside.

Unroll pastry and lay flat; cut sheets in half crosswise. Brush a half-sheet with butter, keeping remaining fila covered with plastic wrap, and then cut half-sheet lengthwise into thirds. Place about 1½ teaspoons of the filling in an upper corner of each strip, fold corner down over filling, and then fold triangle over onto itself, continuing down length of strip.

Place triangles about 1½ inches apart on greased baking sheets, brush with butter, and cover with plastic wrap while shaping remaining triangles. (At this point, you may freeze until firm; then carefully stack in a rigid container, placing foil between layers, cover, and freeze for up to a month. Do not thaw before baking.)

Bake in a 375° oven until well browned and crisp (about 10 minutes; about 35 minutes if frozen). Serve hot or at room temperature. Makes 3 dozen appetizers.

Shrimp & Feta Cheese Filling. Mix 6 ounces **feta cheese,** crumbled; ½ pound **small cooked shrimp;** ⅛ teaspoon *each* **ground white pepper** and **dill weed;** and ¼ cup chopped **parsley.**

Per appetizer: 51 calories, 2 g protein, 2 g carbohydrates, 4 g total fat, 23 mg cholesterol, 106 mg sodium

COCKTAIL TURNOVERS

Preparation time: About 45 minutes, plus at least 4 hours to chill pastry
Cooking time: About 25 minutes

Offer a platter of these miniature, meat-filled triangles for an inviting and elegant light nibble with your favorite beverage.

Cream Cheese Pastry (recipe follows)
1 **small potato (about 5 oz.), finely chopped**
1 **small onion, finely chopped**
½ **pound lean ground beef**
1 **clove garlic, minced or pressed**
¼ **teaspoon** *each* **dry marjoram leaves and pepper**
½ **teaspoon dry oregano leaves**
1 **teaspoon salt**
1 **egg yolk beaten with 2 tablespoons milk**

Prepare Cream Cheese Pastry.

Mix potato, onion, beef, garlic, marjoram, pepper, oregano, and salt; set aside.

On a floured board, roll pastry into a rectangle ⅛ inch thick; cut into 2½-inch squares (you should have about 48). Place 1 teaspoon of the meat filling on each square. Fold dough over to make a triangle, seal edges with a fork, and brush with egg mixture. Arrange on baking sheets. Bake in a 350° oven until golden brown (about 25 minutes). Makes about 4 dozen appetizers.

Cream Cheese Pastry. Beat 1 large package (8 oz.) **cream cheese** and 1 cup (½ lb.) **butter** or margarine, both at room temperature, until smooth. Beat in ½ teaspoon **salt.** Slowly mix in 2 cups **all-purpose flour** to make a stiff dough. Cover with plastic wrap and refrigerate for at least 4 hours or until next day.

Per appetizer: 86 calories, 2 g protein, 5 g carbohydrates, 7 g total fat, 24 mg cholesterol, 126 mg sodium

EMPANADAS

Preparation time: About 30 minutes
Cooking time: About 45 minutes

Bite-size turnovers are filled with a sweet-tart meat and raisin mixture.

Cornmeal Pastry (recipe follows)
1 **teaspoon butter or margarine**
½ **pound** *each* **ground beef and ground pork**
1 **large clove garlic, minced or pressed**
½ **cup** *each* **tomato purée and raisins**
¼ **cup dry sherry**
2 **teaspoons ground cinnamon**
½ **teaspoon ground cloves**
2 **tablespoons vinegar**
1 **tablespoon sugar**
¾ **cup slivered almonds**

Prepare Cornmeal Pastry. While pastry is chilling, melt butter in a wide frying pan over medium heat. Crumble meat into pan and cook, stirring, until no longer pink (about 7 minutes). Drain off fat. Add garlic, tomato purée, raisins, sherry, cinnamon, cloves, vinegar, and sugar. Cook, stirring, until most of the liquid has evaporated (about 20 minutes). Stir in almonds; let cool.

On a floured board, roll pastry ⅛ inch thick. Cut into 3-inch rounds. Evenly spoon meat filling into each circle. Moisten edges with water, fold over, and seal with a fork. Arrange on baking sheets. Bake in a 400° oven until golden brown (about 15 minutes). Makes about 40 appetizers.

Cornmeal Pastry. Mix 2 cups **all-purpose flour,** 1 cup **yellow cornmeal,** 1 tablespoon **baking powder,** and ½ teaspoon **salt.** Cut in ¼ cup cold **butter** or margarine until mixture resembles coarse meal. Beat 1 **egg** and ¾ cup **milk;** with a fork, stir into flour mixture until dough holds together. Gather dough into a ball and knead lightly. Cover and refrigerate for 30 minutes.

Per appetizer: 102 calories, 4 g protein, 11 g carbohydrates, 5 g total fat, 17 mg cholesterol, 95 mg sodium

HOT SPICED APPLE CRÊPES

Preparation time: About 20 minutes
Cooking time: About 10 minutes

Take advantage of purchased crêpes to make this sweet autumn treat. Tart apples laced with rum make a tempting filling.

1 **package (4 oz.) frozen prepared crêpes (6-in. diameter)**
1 **tablespoon butter or margarine**
About 2½ pounds tart apples, such as Granny Smith or Newtown Pippins, peeled, cored, and thinly sliced
1 **tablespoon lemon juice**
1½ **teaspoons apple pie spice**
About ⅓ cup sugar
2 **tablespoons rum or brandy (optional)**

Place crêpes in a baking pan. Cover and bake in a 300° oven until crêpes are warm and easy to separate (about 10 minutes).

Meanwhile, melt butter in a wide frying pan over medium heat. Add apples, lemon juice, and apple pie spice. Cook, turning occasionally, until apples are just tender when pierced (about 4 minutes). Add sugar to taste. Continue cooking, mixing gently, until juices are syrupy (about 3 more minutes).

Drizzle with rum, if desired, and set aflame (not beneath an exhaust fan or near flammable items), shaking pan gently until flames subside. Continue cooking until most of the liquid has evaporated.

Evenly spoon filling onto a quarter of each crêpe; fold crêpes in half and then in half again. Makes 10 appetizers.

Per appetizer: 116 calories, 2 g protein, 25 g carbohydrates, 2 g total fat, 3 mg cholesterol, 30 mg sodium

Appetizer Pizza Squares (recipe on facing page) are a party success story. Simply cut the crisp crust topped with tomato sauce, cheese, artichokes, and salami into bite-size snacks.

Pictured on facing page

APPETIZER PIZZA SQUARES

◆

**Preparation time: About 30 minutes
Cooking time: About 1 hour**

Refrigerated dough cuts down on preparation time for this artichoke-topped pizza, sure to be a party favorite.

 Fresh Tomato Sauce (recipe follows)
1 **jar (6 oz.) marinated artichoke hearts**
2 **packages (10 oz. *each*) refrigerated pizza crust**
3 **cups (12 oz.) shredded whole-milk mozzarella cheese**
¼ **cup grated Parmesan cheese**
¼ **pound thinly sliced dry salami, cut into ½-inch-wide strips**

Prepare Fresh Tomato Sauce.

Meanwhile, drain artichokes, reserving marinade, and coarsely chop. Roll or pat crusts to fit into two 12-inch greased pizza pans (or one 17-inch pan). Brush dough with some of the reserved marinade. Spread with tomato sauce and sprinkle evenly with mozzarella and Parmesan. Evenly distribute artichokes and salami over top.

Bake on lowest rack of a 425° oven until crust is well browned (about 15 minutes for small pizzas, 25 minutes for large). Cut into about 2-inch pieces. Makes about 40 appetizers.

Fresh Tomato Sauce. Heat 2 tablespoons **olive oil** in a 2-quart pan over medium heat. Add 1 small **onion,** finely chopped, and cook, stirring often, until soft (about 7 minutes). Mix in 1 clove **garlic,** minced or pressed; 5 **pear-shaped tomatoes** (about ¾ lb. *total*), peeled and finely chopped; ¼ teaspoon *each* **salt** and **dry oregano leaves;** ½ teaspoon **dry basil leaves;** and ¼ cup **dry white wine.** Bring to a boil; reduce heat, cover, and simmer for 20 minutes. Uncover and cook over medium-high heat, stirring often, until reduced to about 1 cup (about 15 more minutes).

Per appetizer: 86 calories, 4 g protein, 7 g carbohydrates, 4 g total fat, 9 mg cholesterol, 198 mg sodium

PESTO HOTS

◆

**Preparation time: About 10 minutes
Cooking time: About 3 minutes**

This easy appetizer is ready to enjoy in minutes. Simply spread baguette slices with a basil-accented mayonnaise and brown under the broiler.

½ **cup *each* slivered fresh basil leaves and grated Parmesan cheese**
1 **small clove garlic, minced or pressed**
 About 6 tablespoons mayonnaise
1 **small French baguette (8 oz.), sliced ¼ inch thick**

Stir together basil, Parmesan, garlic, and 6 tablespoons of the mayonnaise until well blended; add more mayonnaise, if necessary, to make a firm spreading consistency. Set aside.

Arrange bread slices in a single layer on a large baking sheet. Broil about 4 inches below heat until toasted on top (about 1 minute). Remove from broiler, turn, and spread untoasted sides with mayonnaise mixture, spreading to edges. Continue broiling until bubbling and lightly browned (about 2 more minutes). Makes 2 dozen appetizers.

Per appetizer: 59 calories, 2 g protein, 5 g carbohydrates, 3 g total fat, 4 mg cholesterol, 101 mg sodium

HERBED CHEESE CROUTONS

◆

**Preparation time: About 20 minutes
Cooking time: About 12 minutes**

Watch these golden cheese cubes disappear as soon as you serve them hot from the oven. Try both versions for different flavor sensations.

 About ⅓ of a 1-pound loaf unsliced day-old French bread
½ **to ¾ cup grated Parmesan or Romano cheese**
½ **cup (¼ lb.) butter or margarine, cut into pieces**
1 **clove garlic, minced or pressed**
¼ **teaspoon *each* dry thyme leaves, dry rosemary, summer savory, and paprika**

Slice bread about 1 inch thick; trim and discard crusts. Then cut into 1-inch cubes. Place cheese in a shallow bowl.

In an 8- to 10-inch frying pan, melt butter over low heat. Stir in garlic, thyme, rosemary, summer savory, and paprika; remove from heat. Dip bread cubes into butter mixture to coat on all sides; then roll in cheese.

Arrange in a single layer in a 10-by 15-inch baking pan. Bake in a 350° oven until crisp and golden brown (about 10 minutes). Makes about 2 dozen appetizers.

Per appetizer: 60 calories, 1 g protein, 3 g carbohydrates, 5 g total fat, 12 mg cholesterol, 112 mg sodium

Italian Herbed Cheese Croutons

Follow directions for **Herbed Cheese Croutons,** but omit rosemary, summer savory, and paprika. Instead, add ½ teaspoon **dry basil leaves** and ¼ teaspoon **dry oregano leaves.**

Per appetizer: 60 calories, 1 g protein, 3 g carbohydrates, 5 g total fat, 12 mg cholesterol, 112 mg sodium

SATISFYING SANDWICHES

A very versatile food, sandwiches can play many supporting roles—as hearty appetizers, between-meal snacks, or light meal starters. Different breads, fillings, serving temperatures, and styles make for an almost infinite variety of tastes.

Sandwiches can even announce the theme of a party, a special cuisine, or a certain mood. Whether you choose Olive Relish Poor Boy Sandwich Loaf for an on-the-go picnic, Spiedini alla Romana to begin an Italian feast, or Grilled Ham & Brie on Rye for easy snacking, our sandwiches are sure to please.

EGG & ONION TRIANGLES

Preparation time: About 10 minutes
Cooking time: About 3 minutes
Chilling time: At least 2 hours

Dense, dark pumpernickel is the perfect host for mustardy egg salad. Tart-sweet onions provide a flavorful finish.

> Pink Onions (recipe follows)
> 4 hard-cooked eggs, finely chopped
> 3 tablespoons sour cream
> 2 teaspoons *each* Dijon mustard and mayonnaise
> 1 teaspoon chopped fresh dill or ¼ teaspoon dill weed
> Salt and pepper
> 4 slices thin, dense-textured pumpernickel bread
> 2 green onions (including tops), thinly sliced

Prepare Pink Onions.

Mix eggs, sour cream, mustard, mayonnaise, and dill. Season to taste with salt and pepper. Evenly spread on bread slices. Cut each bread slice diagonally into quarters. Evenly mound Pink Onions over egg mix-

ture. Sprinkle with green onions. Makes 16 snack sandwiches.

Pink Onions. Thinly slice 1 small **red onion** (4 to 6 oz.). In a 1- to 1½-quart pan, bring 1½ cups **water** and 1 tablespoon **vinegar** to a boil over high heat. Add onion, pushing down to submerge. Return to a boil; then drain and place in a bowl. Stir in 2 teaspoons **salad oil**, 1 teaspoon **white wine vinegar**, and ¼ teaspoon *each* **dill seeds** and **mustard seeds.** Cover and refrigerate for at least 2 hours or until next day.

Per sandwich: 58 calories, 3 g protein, 5 g carbohydrates, 3 g total fat, 55 mg cholesterol, 85 mg sodium

RICE CAKES WITH RICOTTA-APRICOT PURÉE

Preparation time: About 15 minutes
Cooking time: About 1 minute (optional)

Rice cakes replace bread in these bite-size, ginger-spiced sandwiches. If desired, lightly broil them just before serving.

> 1 cup dried apricots
> 1 pound ricotta cheese
> 4 teaspoons honey
> ½ teaspoon ground ginger
> 36 miniature rice cakes (2-in. diameter)

Thinly sliver 6 of the apricots; reserve for garnish. Whirl remaining apricots in a food processor until minced. Add ricotta, honey, and ginger; whirl

until puréed. (Or mince apricots with a knife. Then beat with ricotta, honey, and ginger until blended.)

Evenly spread apricot mixture on rice cakes. Garnish with apricot slivers. Serve cold. Or, to serve warm, arrange in a single layer on a 12- by 15-inch baking sheet and broil about 4 inches below heat just until mixture begins to brown (about 1 minute). Makes 3 dozen snack sandwiches.

Per sandwich: 36 calories, 2 g protein, 5 g carbohydrates, .9 g total fat, 4 mg cholesterol, 18 mg sodium

GRILLED HAM & BRIE ON RYE

Preparation time: About 5 minutes
Cooking time: About 5 minutes

Rich-tasting Brie grilled with ham and slivered sweet onion lifts these ham and cheese sandwiches out of the ordinary.

> 8 slices sourdough rye or regular rye bread
> 8 thin slices Black Forest ham (7 oz. *total*)
> ½ pound firm-ripe Brie cheese, sliced
> ½ small red onion, thinly slivered

Make 4 sandwiches, using 2 slices of the bread, 2 slices of the ham, a quarter of the Brie, and a quarter of the onion for each.

Place a ridged grill pan, griddle, or wide frying pan over low heat until a drop of water dances on surface. Place sandwiches in pan. Cook, turning once, until browned on both sides (about 5 minutes). Cut each sandwich in half and serve hot. Makes 8 snack sandwiches.

Per sandwich: 201 calories, 14 g protein, 14 g carbohydrates, 10 g total fat, 43 mg cholesterol, 690 mg sodium

SPICED LENTILS IN POCKET BREADS

Preparation time: About 15 minutes
Cooking time: About 40 minutes

Pocket breads make handy holders for lentils mixed with chile, bay leaf, and cumin. Top with minty yogurt.

- 1 cup (7 oz.) lentils
- 1 quart water
- 1 bay leaf
- 1 small dried hot red chile
- 1 teaspoon cumin seeds
- ⅓ cup olive oil
- 3 tablespoons wine vinegar
- 1 clove garlic, minced or pressed
- ½ cup thinly sliced green onions (including tops)
- 1 cup chopped celery
  Salt and pepper
  Yogurt Sauce (recipe follows)
- 4 pocket bread rounds (6-in. diameter), cut in half

Sort lentils and discard any debris; rinse well and drain. Place in 3- to 4-quart pan with water, bay leaf, chile, and cumin seeds. Bring to a boil over high heat; reduce heat, cover, and simmer just until lentils are tender (about 40 minutes). Drain and let cool. Discard chile.

In a large bowl, mix oil, vinegar, and garlic; stir in lentils. (At this point, you may cover and refrigerate until next day.)

Just before serving, stir in onions and celery. Season to taste with salt and pepper.

Prepare Yogurt Sauce. Evenly spoon lentil mixture into each pocket bread half and offer with sauce. Makes 8 snack sandwiches.

Per sandwich: 257 calories, 10 g protein, 34 g carbohydrates, 9 g total fat, 0 mg cholesterol, 199 mg sodium

Yogurt Sauce. Mix 1 cup **plain yogurt,** 2 tablespoons chopped **fresh mint leaves,** and 2 tablespoons **golden raisins.** Makes 1¼ cups.

Per tablespoon: 10 calories, .6 g protein, 2 g carbohydrates, .2 g total fat, .7 mg cholesterol, 8 mg sodium

OLIVE RELISH POOR BOY SANDWICH LOAF

Preparation time: About 10 minutes

Fill a loaf of sourdough bread with salami, turkey, and Swiss cheese, and you have a hearty sandwich. Add two kinds of olives in a lemony vinaigrette, and you have a heroic one.

- ¼ cup olive oil
- 1½ tablespoons red wine vinegar
- 1 teaspoon grated lemon peel
- 1 clove garlic, minced or pressed
- ⅛ teaspoon coarsely ground pepper
- ½ cup *each* chopped ripe olives and pimento-stuffed green olives
- 1 long loaf sourdough French bread (1 lb.)
- 4 to 6 butter lettuce leaves, washed and crisped
- ¼ pound thinly sliced dry salami
- 6 ounces *each* thinly sliced cooked turkey breast and Swiss cheese
  Red onion rings (optional)

Mix oil, vinegar, lemon peel, garlic, and pepper until well combined; stir in olives. Set aside.

Split bread in half lengthwise; pull out bread from top half, leaving about a ½-inch-thick shell (reserve crumbs for other uses).

Spread cut surfaces of both bread halves with olive mixture. Cover bottom half with lettuce leaves. Add salami, turkey, and cheese. Top with onion, if desired. Cover with top half of loaf.

Fasten sandwich at 2-inch intervals with wooden picks. Cut between picks. Makes 8 snack sandwiches.

Per sandwich: 382 calories, 20 g protein, 25 g carbohydrates, 22 g total fat, 47 mg cholesterol, 848 mg sodium

SPIEDINI ALLA ROMANA

Preparation time: About 15 minutes
Cooking time: About 20 minutes

Ham and cheese Italian style means prosciutto and mozzarella on Italian bread. Lightly battered and fried until golden, spiedini are served crisp and hot.

- 8 thin slices Italian or French bread, crusts trimmed
- 4 slices mozzarella cheese (about 2 oz. *total*)
- 8 thin slices prosciutto (about 3 oz. *total*)
- ¾ cup milk
- ⅓ cup all-purpose flour
- 2 eggs, lightly beaten
- ⅓ cup olive or salad oil

Make 4 sandwiches, using 2 slices of the bread, 1 slice of the cheese, and 2 slices of the prosciutto for each. Cut each into quarters and fasten with wooden picks. Place milk, flour, and eggs in separate shallow bowls.

Heat oil in an 8- to 10-inch frying pan over medium heat. Lightly dip each sandwich, coating all sides, in milk, then in flour, and finally in eggs. Cook sandwiches, a few at a time, turning once, until crusty and golden (about 5 minutes). Makes 16 snack sandwiches.

Per sandwich: 97 calories, 4 g protein, 5 g carbohydrates, 7 g total fat, 34 mg cholesterol, 168 mg sodium

Pictured on front cover

CHEESE WAFERS

◆

Preparation time: About 20 minutes
Cooking time: About 10 minutes

Sharp Cheddar cheese combines with dry mustard and ground red pepper to make a savory cracker.

⅔ **cup butter or margarine, at room temperature**
½ **cup shredded sharp Cheddar cheese**
1 **egg**
⅛ **teaspoon ground red pepper (cayenne)**
¼ **teaspoon dry mustard**
½ **teaspoon** *each* **salt and sugar**
1⅔ **cups all-purpose flour**

Beat butter and cheese. Add egg, pepper, mustard, salt, and sugar; beat until well blended. Gradually add flour, stirring until smooth. Shape dough into a ball.

Place dough, about half at a time, in a cooky press fitted with a sawtooth pattern and shape wafers, cutting at 1-inch intervals, on baking sheets. Bake in a 375° oven until golden (about 10 minutes). Serve warm or at room temperature. Makes about 4 dozen appetizers.

Per appetizer: 45 calories, .9 g protein, 3 g carbohydrates, 3 g total fat, 13 mg cholesterol, 58 mg sodium

Sesame Cheese Wafers

Follow directions for **Cheese Wafers,** but instead of cutting dough with a cooky press, divide dough in half and shape each portion into a smooth log about 1½ inches in diameter. For each portion, sprinkle 1½ tablespoons **sesame seeds** on wax paper. Roll log in seeds, pressing in lightly. Wrap in wax paper or plastic wrap

and refrigerate for at least 2 hours or until next day.

Slice dough about ¼ inch thick and arrange rounds slightly apart on baking sheets. Bake as directed. Makes about 5 dozen appetizers.

Per appetizer: 39 calories, .8 g protein, 3 g carbohydrates, 3 g total fat, 10 mg cholesterol, 46 mg sodium

BABY DUTCH BABIES

◆

Preparation time: About 15 minutes
Cooking time: About 15 minutes

Petite Dutch babies, a close relative of popovers, cradle a savory filling of cream cheese and chutney.

2 **tablespoons butter or margarine**
2 **eggs**
½ **cup** *each* **all-purpose flour and milk**
1 **small package (3 oz.) cream cheese**
¼ **cup chutney, chopped**

Divide butter evenly among twenty-four 1½-inch or twelve 2½-inch muffin cups. Place in a 425° oven until butter is melted (about 3 minutes).

Meanwhile, whirl eggs, flour, and milk in a food processor or blender until smooth. Cut cheese into cubes to equal number of muffin cups; set aside.

Evenly spoon batter into cups. Bake until bottoms are firm (2 minutes for small cups, 5 minutes for large cups). Remove from oven and quickly add 1 piece of the cheese and ½ teaspoon (for small cups) or 1 teaspoon (for large cups) of the chutney to each cup. Return to oven and continue baking until puffed (about 10 more minutes).

Let cool briefly; then remove from pans. Serve warm or at room temperature. Makes 2 dozen small or 1 dozen large appetizers.

Per appetizer (small): 46 calories, 1 g protein, 4 g carbohydrates, 3 g total fat, 25 mg cholesterol, 34 mg sodium

Pictured on facing page

CHEESE TWISTS

◆

Preparation time: About 30 minutes
Cooking time: About 10 minutes

Light, flaky, and buttery—that's how to describe these cheese sticks, perfect openers for a sophisticated evening. Top the twists with sesame or poppy seeds.

1 **cup all-purpose flour**
½ **teaspoon** *each* **salt and ground ginger**
⅓ **cup butter or margarine**
1 **cup (4 oz.) shredded sharp Cheddar cheese**
½ **teaspoon Worcestershire**
2 **to 2½ tablespoons cold water**
1 **egg, beaten**
1 **tablespoon** *each* **sesame and poppy seeds**

Mix flour, salt, and ginger. Cut in butter until mixture resembles fine crumbs. Stir in cheese. Add Worcestershire to 1 tablespoon of the water and sprinkle over flour mixture. Mix lightly, adding remaining water as needed, until dough holds together. Shape into a flattened ball.

On a lightly floured board, roll dough into a 10-inch square. Brush with egg and cut in half. Sprinkle sesame seeds on 1 portion and poppy seeds on other portion. Then cut each portion into ½- by 5-inch strips. Holding each strip at ends, twist in opposite directions. Place about 1 inch apart on greased baking sheets.

Bake in a 400° oven until golden brown (about 10 minutes). Serve warm or at room temperature. Makes 40 appetizers.

Per appetizer: 41 calories, 1 g protein, 3 g carbohydrates, 3 g total fat, 12 mg cholesterol, 63 mg sodium

Let guests picnic on shallot- and sausage-accented Rice-stuffed Summer Squash (recipe on page 68), Spicy Chicken Wings (recipe on page 52) with blue cheese dip, and delicate Cheese Twists (recipe on facing page) topped with sesame and poppy seeds.

ZUCCHINI MADELEINES

Preparation time: About 30 minutes
Cooking time: About 25 minutes

This moist, cheese-laced variation on the French dessert cooky adds zucchini for texture and flavor. Serve right from the oven or at room temperature.

    3 medium-size zucchini (about
       1 lb. *total*), shredded
    2 teaspoons salt
    6 tablespoons olive oil
    1 medium-size onion, chopped
    1 cup all-purpose flour
    1 tablespoon baking powder
    5 eggs
    2 tablespoons milk
 1½ cups (about 6 oz.) freshly grated
       Parmesan cheese
    1 clove garlic, minced or pressed
    2 tablespoons chopped fresh basil
       leaves or 1 teaspoon dry basil
       leaves
    ¼ teaspoon pepper

Mix zucchini with salt. Let stand until zucchini is limp and liquid has drained from it (about 30 minutes). Rinse well and drain, squeezing out as much water as possible.

Meanwhile, heat 2 tablespoons of the oil in an 8- to 10-inch frying pan over medium-high heat. Add onion and cook, stirring, until soft (about 7 minutes); set aside.

In a large bowl, mix flour and baking powder. In another bowl, whisk eggs, milk, remaining 4 tablespoons oil, cheese, garlic, basil, and pepper until blended; add zucchini and onion and mix well. Stir into flour mixture just until evenly moistened.

Spoon batter into greased and floured madeleine pans (1½- or 2-tablespoon size) or tiny muffin pans (about 1½-in. diameter), filling to rims. Bake in a 400° oven until puffed and lightly browned (about 15 minutes for 1½-tablespoon size, 18 minutes for 2-tablespoon size, 20 minutes for small muffins). Let cool for 5 minutes; then invert pans to remove. Serve hot or at room temperature.

If made ahead, let cool completely, wrap airtight, and refrigerate until next day; freeze for longer storage. To reheat, lay madeleines (thawed, if frozen) in a single layer on baking sheets and place in a 350° oven until warm (about 5 minutes). Makes about 3 dozen appetizers.

Per appetizer: 65 calories, 3 g protein, 4 g carbohydrates, 4 g total fat, 33 mg cholesterol, 151 mg sodium

QUICK SALT STICKS

Preparation time: About 15 minutes
Cooking time: About 15 minutes

Take advantage of frozen puff pastry to make simple salt sticks, perfect for nibbling with dips and spreads. The sticks can be made ahead, chilled, and heated just before serving.

    1 package (17¼ oz.) frozen puff
       pastry, thawed
 1½ teaspoons caraway seeds
    1 egg white, lightly beaten
    1 teaspoon coarse (kosher-style)
       salt

Unfold pastry sheets and cut each into quarters; then cut each quarter into 2 triangles. Sprinkle evenly with caraway seeds.

Starting with longest side, roll each triangle into a stick. Place, center points down and several inches apart, on a 12- by 15-inch baking sheet. Brush lightly with egg white; sprinkle evenly with salt. Bake in a 400° oven until golden brown (about 15 minutes).

If made ahead, let cool on racks, wrap airtight, and refrigerate until next day. To reheat, lay on a baking sheet and place in a 400° oven until hot (about 5 minutes). Makes 16 appetizers.

Per appetizer: 132 calories, 2 g protein, 11 g carbohydrates, 9 g total fat, 0 mg cholesterol, 241 mg sodium

Pictured on front cover
POLENTA TRIANGLES

Preparation time: About 10 minutes
Cooking time: About 18 minutes

Polenta, coarsely ground cornmeal traditionally used in Italian cooking, adds crunch to buttery flatbread triangles. Use freshly grated Parmesan cheese to give extra flavor to the cornbread, delicious alone or as a carrier for a dip or spread.

    ⅔ cup polenta or yellow cornmeal
    1 cup all-purpose flour
    ½ cup (¼ lb.) butter or margarine
    ½ cup freshly grated Parmesan
       cheese
    1 egg
    ¼ cup milk

In a food processor or bowl, combine polenta, flour, butter, and cheese. Whirl or rub with your fingers until mixture forms fine crumbs. Add egg and milk; whirl or stir just until moistened. Pat dough into a greased 9- by 13-inch pan.

Bake in a 400° oven until golden brown (about 18 minutes). Cut into about 2-inch squares; then cut each square diagonally in half. If made ahead, cool, cover, and let stand until next day. Makes 4 dozen appetizers.

Per appetizer: 40 calories, 1 g protein, 4 g carbohydrates, 2 g total fat, 10 mg cholesterol, 37 mg sodium

SLICED PEPPER STEAK IN MUSTARD SAUCE

◆

Preparation time: About 5 minutes
Cooking time: About 10 minutes

Barbecue a thick sirloin steak encrusted with peppercorns; then slice thinly, swirl in a mustardy butter sauce, and serve on sliced French bread.

- 2 teaspoons freeze-dried green peppercorns, coarsely crushed
- 1 pound top sirloin steak (about 1 in. thick), trimmed of fat
- 2 tablespoons butter or margarine
- 1 tablespoon Dijon mustard
- 1 tablespoon dry vermouth or dry white wine
- 1 small French baguette (8 oz.), sliced ½ inch thick

Sprinkle peppercorns over both sides of steak, pressing in lightly. Place steak on a lightly greased grill 4 to 6 inches above a solid bed of hot coals. (Or place steak on a rack in a broiler pan and broil about 3 inches below heat.) Cook, turning once, until done to your liking when cut (about 10 minutes for medium-rare).

Meanwhile, melt butter in a 3- to 4-cup pan on cooler part of grill (or over low heat); stir in mustard and vermouth.

Transfer steak to a rimmed platter; pour sauce over and around steak. Cut into thin, slanting slices, swirling pieces in sauce. Offer with bread slices. Makes 1 dozen appetizers.

Per appetizer: 123 calories, 9 g protein, 11 g carbohydrates, 5 g total fat, 26 mg cholesterol, 182 mg sodium

GINGERY MARINATED BEEF CUBES

◆

Preparation time: About 5 minutes
Marinating time: At least 2 hours
Cooking time: About 7 minutes

Enjoy the gingery, peppery seasonings of this tender beef appetizer. Marinate the meat up to a day ahead; then quickly stir-fry the bite-size pieces.

- 1 tablespoon sesame seeds
- ¼ cup soy sauce
- 2 to 3 teaspoons minced fresh ginger
- 3 cloves garlic, minced or pressed
- 1 teaspoon *each* sugar and vinegar
- 2 green onions (including tops), thinly sliced
- ¼ to ½ teaspoon ground red pepper (cayenne)
  About 5 tablespoons salad oil
- 1½ pounds boneless beef sirloin, top round, or boneless chuck, cut into ¾-inch cubes

Toast sesame seeds in a small frying pan over medium heat, shaking pan frequently, until golden (about 3 minutes). In a bowl, mix sesame seeds, soy, ginger, garlic, sugar, vinegar, onions, pepper, and 1 tablespoon of the oil. Add meat, stirring to coat. Cover and refrigerate for at least 2 hours or until next day.

Heat 2 more tablespoons of the oil in a wide frying pan over high heat. Add meat, half at a time, and cook, stirring, until done to your liking when cut (about 2 minutes for medium doneness). Repeat with remaining meat, adding remaining oil as needed.

Offer with wooden picks. Makes about 4 dozen appetizers.

Per appetizer: 59 calories, 3 g protein, .3 g carbohydrates, 5 g total fat, 10 mg cholesterol, 93 mg sodium

BARBECUED PRIME RIB BONES

◆

Preparation time: About 5 minutes
Marinating time: About 2 hours
Cooking time: About 20 minutes

Meaty ribs flavored with a tangy mustard marinade make a hearty opener at an outdoor party.

- **About 6 pounds standing rib bones**
- **Mustard Marinade (recipe follows)**

Arrange meat in a large shallow baking pan. Prepare Mustard Marinade and pour over ribs; turn to coat. Cover and let stand for about 2 hours.

Lift ribs from marinade, reserving marinade. Place on a lightly greased grill 4 to 6 inches above a solid bed of hot coals. (Or place ribs in a 10- by 15-inch baking pan and bake in a 425° oven.) Cook, turning frequently and brushing with marinade, until done to your liking when cut (about 20 minutes for medium-rare).

Cut between bones to separate ribs. Makes about 1 dozen appetizers.

Mustard Marinade. Combine ⅓ cup **Dijon mustard** and 2 tablespoons **red wine vinegar**. Beating constantly with a wire whisk, add ¼ cup **olive** or salad **oil**, a few drops at a time. Beat in 1 clove **garlic**, minced or pressed; ½ teaspoon *each* **dry thyme leaves** and **Worcestershire**; and ¼ teaspoon **pepper**.

Per appetizer: 322 calories, 15 g protein, 1 g carbohydrates, 28 g total fat, 60 mg cholesterol, 245 mg sodium

Begin a backyard barbecue with richly basted Down-home Baby Back Ribs (recipe on facing page), crispy coated Parmesan Zucchini Sticks (recipe on page 69), and tangy fresh Artichoke Hearts with Blue Cheese (recipe on page 63).

BEEF CHIANG MAI

Preparation time: About 10 minutes
Cooking time: About 12 minutes

Cool, crisp lettuce leaves hold a warm, spicy beef mixture in this traditional dish from northern Thailand. Have your guests wrap their own meat bundles after topping them with sprigs of mint.

- ¼ cup short- or long-grain rice
- 1 pound lean ground beef
- 1 teaspoon *each* sugar and crushed red pepper
- ½ cup *each* thinly sliced green onions (including tops) and chopped fresh mint leaves
- 2 tablespoons chopped cilantro (coriander)
- ¼ cup lemon juice
- 1½ tablespoons soy sauce
  Small inner leaves from 2 large or 3 small heads butter lettuce, washed and crisped
  About 36 fresh mint sprigs

Place a wide frying pan or wok over medium heat. When pan is hot, add rice and cook, stirring, until golden (about 5 minutes). Remove from heat and transfer to a blender or food processor; whirl until finely ground. Set aside.

Return pan to heat. When wok is hot, crumble in beef and cook, stirring, until no longer pink (about 7 minutes). Stir in rice, sugar, pepper, onions, chopped mint, cilantro, lemon juice, and soy. Pour into a dish and surround with lettuce leaves and mint sprigs.

Spoon beef mixture onto lettuce leaves, top with a mint sprig, and roll up. Makes about 3 dozen appetizers.

Per appetizer: 124 calories, 7 g protein, 5 g carbohydrates, 8 g total fat, 28 mg cholesterol, 157 mg sodium

CRANBERRY COCKTAIL MEATBALLS

Preparation time: About 25 minutes
Cooking time: About 5 minutes

Just because these bite-size meatballs are served in cranberry sauce doesn't mean you have to save them for the holidays. Guests will enjoy their zesty flavor anytime, and you'll appreciate the ease of baking rather than sautéing them.

- 2 pounds lean ground beef
- 1 cup cornflake crumbs
- ⅓ cup finely chopped parsley
- 2 eggs, lightly beaten
- ¼ teaspoon pepper
- 1 clove garlic, minced or pressed
- ⅓ cup catsup
- 2 tablespoons *each* thinly sliced green onions (including tops) and soy sauce
- 1 can (1 lb.) whole berry cranberry sauce
- 1 bottle (12 oz.) tomato-based chili sauce
- 1 tablespoon *each* brown sugar and lemon juice

Thoroughly mix beef, cornflake crumbs, parsley, eggs, pepper, garlic, catsup, onions, and soy; shape into 1-inch balls (you should have about 75). Arrange, slightly apart, in shallow 10- by 15-inch baking pans. Bake in a 500° oven until lightly browned (about 5 minutes).

Meanwhile, in a 2- to 3-quart pan, cook cranberry sauce, chili sauce, sugar, and lemon juice over medium heat, stirring, until bubbling (about 3 minutes).

With a slotted spoon, transfer meatballs to a warm serving dish; pour sauce over meatballs. Offer with wooden picks. Makes about 75 appetizers.

Per appetizer: 48 calories, 3 g protein, 5 g carbohydrates, 2 g total fat, 13 mg cholesterol, 128 mg sodium

Pictured on facing page
DOWN-HOME BABY BACK RIBS

Preparation time: About 5 minutes
Cooking time: About 1 hour and 10 minutes

Pork spareribs are a perennial favorite, perfect for backyard barbecues with family and friends. A traditional molasses and catsup sauce accents the tender, juicy meat.

- 4 pounds pork spareribs (preferably baby back ribs)
- ½ cup water
- ¼ cup *each* catsup and light molasses
- 2 tablespoons soy sauce
- 2 cloves garlic, minced or pressed
- 1 teaspoon *each* dry mustard and ground ginger

Place ribs, overlapping slightly if necessary, in a 12- by 17-inch roasting pan; add water. Cover and bake in a 350° oven until tender when pierced (about 1 hour).

Shortly before ribs are done, combine catsup, molasses, soy, garlic, mustard, and ginger in a 1- to 1½-quart pan. Cook over medium heat, stirring, until hot; set aside.

Drain ribs, discarding liquid from baking pan. Brush all over with sauce. Place on a lightly greased grill 4 to 6 inches above a solid bed of medium coals. (Or place ribs on a rack in a broiler pan and broil about 4 inches below heat.) Cook, turning occasionally and brushing with remaining sauce, until well browned (about 10 minutes).

Cut between bones to separate. Makes about 1 dozen appetizers.

Per appetizer: 261 calories, 17 g protein, 6 g carbohydrates, 18 g total fat, 71 mg cholesterol, 287 mg sodium

APPETIZING MENUS

Planning a party can be fun, especially when you choose a particular theme or celebrate a special occasion. When deciding on your appetizers, think about the taste, texture, temperature, and color of your choices, as well as the weather, time of day, and other food you'll be serving.

The menus we've created include spreads that showcase a particular ethnic cuisine, starters for an elegant dinner party, basic beginners for a lazy summer supper, and even hors d'oeuvres you can make with ingredients you have on hand when unexpected guests drop by.

To determine how many appetizers you'll need, follow the guidelines in "Great Beginnings" on pages 4–5.

ELEGANT EVENING

Melted Brie with Winter Fruits, page 18

Turkey Rillettes, page 28

Zucchini Madeleines, page 44

Heavenly Mushrooms, page 64

Twice-baked Creamers, page 66

Tomato Tarts Niçoise, page 74

SPUR–OF–THE MOMENT PARTY

Hummus, page 15

Curried Raisins, Peanuts & Banana Chips, page 25

Quick Tuna-Anchovy Spread, page 26

Apricot & Almond-Butter Bites, page 81

Needles in a Haystack, page 81

Cherry Tomatoes with Smoked Oysters, page 84

Orange-Fennel Olives, page 92

ORIENTAL BANQUET

Asian Eggplant Dip, page 13

Gingery Marinated Beef Cubes, page 45

Chicken Yakitori, page 52

Phoenix-tail Shrimp, page 60

Marbled Tea Eggs, page 72

Thai Carrot Salad, page 90

Sesame Long Beans, page 90

SPRINGTIME CELEBRATION

Appetizer Mini-Quiches, page 34

Veal & Olive Terrine, page 76

Spinach-wrapped Chicken, page 77

Asparagus in Belgian Endive, page 87

Minted Peas & Almonds, page 92

Nut- & Cheese-filled Fruits, page 93

TAILGATE PICNIC

Apple Aïoli, page 12

Stuffed Camembert, page 20

Sweet Potato Chips, page 25

Creamy Braunschweiger Appetizer, page 26

Zucchini Frittata, page 73

Lean Terrine, page 79

Steeped Shrimp, page 85

Pickled Cucumbers, page 90

ITALIAN FEAST

Gorgonzola Pesto, page 8

Appetizer Pizza Squares, page 39

Baked Shrimp with Garlic, page 61

Florentine Mushrooms, page 65

Stuffed Pasta Shells Italiano, page 84

Meat-wrapped Fruits, page 93

EASY SUMMER SUPPER

Lazy Liptauer Cheese, page 20

Chili-baked Chicken Wings, page 77

Chilled Cucumber Cream Soup, page 81

Snap Pea Knots, page 92

Fruited Tabbouleh, page 92

Fresh Melon Pickles, page 93

MEXICAN BUFFET

Chile con Queso, page 8

Black Bean Dip, page 15

Salsa Fresca, page 17

Empanadas, page 37

Scallop Seviche, page 79

Jicama & Fresh Fruit Platter, page 93

SUNDAY BRUNCH

Tarragon Mayonnaise, page 10

Potted Shrimp with Chervil, page 26

Scotch Baked Eggs, page 32

Hot Spiced Apple Crêpes, page 37

Baby Dutch Babies, page 42

Turkey-Cheese Pinwheels, page 77

CHINESE PORK APPETIZERS

◆

Preparation time: About 15 minutes
Marinating time: At least 1 hour
Cooking time: About 7 minutes

Cinnamon, cloves, and anise seeds in a soy-based sauce flavor lean boneless pork in this easy, Asian-inspired appetizer.

- ¼ **cup soy sauce**
- 2 **tablespoons salad oil**
- 2 **cloves garlic, minced or pressed**
- 1 **small dried hot red chile, crushed**
- ½ **teaspoon sugar**
- ¼ **teaspoon anise seeds**
- ⅛ **teaspoon** *each* **ground cinnamon and ground cloves**
- 2 **pounds lean boneless pork**

Mix soy, oil, garlic, chile, sugar, anise seeds, cinnamon, and cloves; set aside.

Cut pork into ¼- to ½-inch-thick strips about 1 inch wide (you should have about 48 strips). Add to soy mixture, stirring to coat. Cover and refrigerate for at least 1 hour or up to 2 hours, stirring several times.

Meanwhile, soak 24 bamboo skewers in hot water to cover for 30 minutes.

Thread 2 strips of meat onto each skewer. Place on a lightly greased grill 4 to 6 inches above a solid bed of medium coals. (Or place skewers on a rack in a broiler pan and broil about 4 inches below heat.) Cook, turning occasionally, until no longer pink in center when cut (about 7 minutes). Makes 2 dozen appetizers.

Per appetizer: 74 calories, 9 g protein, .3 g carbohydrates, 4 g total fat, 27 mg cholesterol, 150 mg sodium

---

Pictured on page 62

MEATBALLS WRAPPED IN BASIL LEAVES

◆

Preparation time: About 35 minutes
Cooking time: About 10 minutes

Fresh basil and fennel seeds season grilled meatballs made from pork sausage. Wrap a whole basil leaf around each meatball for extra flavor and eye appeal.

For an alternative with less fat, try the variation using ground turkey.

- 1 **pound bulk pork sausage**
- ½ **cup minced fresh basil leaves**
- 1 **teaspoon crushed fennel seeds**
- 24 **large fresh basil leaves**

Soak 8 bamboo skewers in hot water to cover for 30 minutes.

Meanwhile, thoroughly mix sausage, minced basil, and fennel seeds. Shape into about 1-inch balls (you should have 24). Wrap a basil leaf around each meatball, lightly pressing it into meat so it sticks (leaf does not have to cover entire meatball). Thread 3 meatballs on each skewer.

Place on a greased grill 2 to 4 inches above a solid bed of hot coals. Cook, turning every 2 to 3 minutes, until no longer pink in center when cut (about 10 minutes). Makes 8 appetizers.

Per appetizer: 104 calories, 6 g protein, 1 g carbohydrates, 8 g total fat, 22 mg cholesterol, 349 mg sodium

Turkey Meatballs Wrapped in Basil Leaves

Follow directions for **Meatballs Wrapped in Basil Leaves,** but substitute 1 pound **ground turkey breast** for sausage. Do not grill; instead, place skewers on a rimmed baking sheet. Bake in a 450° oven, turning once, until meat is no longer pink in center when cut (about 8 minutes).

Per appetizer: 70 calories, 13 g protein, 1 g carbohydrates, 1 g total fat, 29 g mg cholesterol, 30 mg sodium

---

MEATBALLS & GINGER GLAZE

◆

Preparation time: About 25 minutes
Cooking time: About 45 minutes

A sweet-sour sauce enlivened by a generous helping of fresh ginger coats meatballs made with ground pork, green onions, and crisp water chestnuts.

- **Ginger Glaze (recipe follows)**
- 1 **can (about 8 oz.) water chestnuts, drained and finely chopped**
- 1 **cup chopped green onions (including tops)**
- 2 **pounds lean ground pork**
- 2 **tablespoons soy sauce**
- 2 **eggs, lightly beaten**
- ¾ **cup fine dry bread crumbs**
  About 1 tablespoon salad oil

Prepare Ginger Glaze; set aside.

Thoroughly mix water chestnuts, onions, pork, soy, eggs, and bread crumbs. Shape into ¾-inch balls (you should have about 72).

Heat 1 tablespoon of the oil in a wide frying pan over medium heat. Add meatballs, about a third at a time, and cook, stirring, until well browned (about 10 minutes); add oil as needed. Remove meatballs and set aside. Clean pan.

Add glaze to pan, increase heat to high, and stir until glaze boils vigorously. Add meatballs, reduce heat, and simmer for 10 minutes. Offer with wooden picks. Makes about 6 dozen appetizers.

Ginger Glaze. Smoothly mix ½ cup **water** and ¼ cup **cornstarch.** Stir in 1 cup *each* **unsweetened pineapple juice** and **regular-strength beef broth,** ½ cup **cider vinegar,** ⅓ cup **sugar,** 1 tablespoon **soy sauce,** and 2 tablespoons minced **fresh ginger.**

Per appetizer: 42 calories, 3 g protein, 3 g carbohydrates, 2 g total fat, 15 mg cholesterol, 71 mg sodium

BARBECUED LAMB RIBS

Preparation time: About 10 minutes
Cooking time: About 25 minutes

Distinctive lamb spareribs grill to juicy tenderness cloaked in a tomato-based barbecue sauce. The ribs can also be broiled, if desired.

- 1 tablespoon olive oil
- ½ cup finely chopped onion
- 1 clove garlic, minced or pressed
- ¼ teaspoon *each* dry oregano leaves and ground cinnamon
- ⅛ teaspoon ground red pepper (cayenne)
- 1½ teaspoons brown sugar
- 1 tablespoon balsamic or cider vinegar
- ¼ cup catsup
- 2 tablespoons dry red wine
- 2 sections (2 to 2½ lbs. *total*) lamb spareribs, trimmed of fat

Heat oil in a 1- to 1½-quart pan over medium heat. Add onion and garlic and cook, stirring often, until soft (about 7 minutes). Add oregano, cinnamon, pepper, sugar, vinegar, catsup, and wine. Increase heat to high and boil, stirring, for 1 minute. Let cool briefly. (At this point, you may cool completely, cover, and refrigerate for up to 2 days.)

Brush ribs with sauce. Place on a lightly greased grill 4 to 6 inches above a solid bed of medium-hot coals. (Or place ribs on a rack in a broiler pan and broil about 3 inches below heat.) Cook, turning once and brushing with any remaining sauce, until browned (about 15 minutes for medium-rare).

Cut between bones to separate. Makes about 1½ dozen appetizers.

Per appetizer: 94 calories, 4 g protein, 2 g carbohydrates, 8 g total fat, 19 mg cholesterol, 49 mg sodium

---

Pictured on facing page

LAMB MEATBALLS WITH PINE NUTS

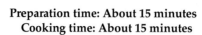

Preparation time: About 15 minutes
Cooking time: About 15 minutes

Meatballs made with ground lamb are covered with a sweet-sour sauce.

- 1 egg, lightly beaten
- ½ teaspoon *each* salt and ground cinnamon
- 1 clove garlic, minced or pressed
- 2 tablespoons *each* fine dry bread crumbs and catsup
- 1 tablespoon red wine vinegar
- ¼ cup pine nuts or slivered almonds
- 1½ pounds lean ground lamb
- 1 tablespoon olive oil
- 1 small red onion, thinly slivered
- ½ cup Marsala or cream sherry
- 2 teaspoons lemon juice
  Chopped parsley (optional)

Mix egg, salt, cinnamon, garlic, bread crumbs, catsup, and vinegar. Add nuts and lamb; mix lightly. Shape into 1-inch balls (you should have about 48). Arrange, slightly apart, in a baking pan. Bake in a 500° oven until well browned (about 10 minutes).

Meanwhile, heat oil in a wide frying pan over medium heat. Add onion and cook, stirring often, until soft (about 10 minutes). Remove pan from heat and set aside.

With a slotted spoon, transfer meatballs to a dish and keep warm. Discard fat from baking pan. Pour a little of the wine into pan, scraping browned bits free; add to onion mixture along with remaining wine and lemon juice. Boil over high heat, stirring, until reduced by about half. Pour over meatballs and sprinkle with parsley, if desired. Offer with wooden picks. Makes about 4 dozen appetizers.

Per appetizer: 42 calories, 3 g protein, .9 g carbohydrates, 3 g total fat, 15 mg cholesterol, 42 mg sodium

---

BLACKBERRY SHISH KEBABS

Preparation time: About 45 minutes
Marinating time: At least 4 hours
Cooking time: About 8 minutes

Blackberry syrup blends with soy sauce and fresh mint to create a complementary marinade for lamb. Grill the meat quickly—browned on the outside, but still pink in the center—for best flavor and texture.

- ½ cup blackberry syrup
- ¼ cup red wine vinegar
- 2 tablespoons *each* soy sauce and chopped fresh mint leaves
- 2 cloves garlic, minced or pressed
- ½ teaspoon pepper
- 2 cans (about 8 oz. *each*) whole water chestnuts, drained
- 1½ pounds lean boneless lamb (leg or shoulder), cut into 1-inch cubes

Mix syrup, vinegar, soy, mint, garlic, and pepper. Add water chestnuts and lamb, stirring to coat. Cover and refrigerate for at least 4 hours or until next day, stirring several times.

Soak 12 bamboo skewers in hot water to cover for 30 minutes. Lift meat and water chestnuts from marinade and thread alternately on skewers (to avoid splitting water chestnuts, rotate skewer as you pierce them).

Place on a lightly greased grill 4 to 6 inches above a solid bed of medium coals. (Or place skewers on a rack in a broiler pan and broil about 4 inches below heat.) Cook, turning occasionally, until meat is browned but still pink in center when cut (about 8 minutes). Makes 1 dozen appetizers.

Per appetizer: 137 calories, 13 g protein, 14 g carbohydrates, 3 g total fat, 38 mg cholesterol, 204 mg sodium

*Welcome special company with cinnamon-accented
Lamb Meatballs with Pine Nuts (recipe on facing page),
savory Peppered Chèvre with Pears (recipe on page 21),
and pungent Garlic-buttered Mushrooms (recipe on
page 64).*

Pictured on page 43

SPICY CHICKEN WINGS

Preparation time: About 15 minutes
Cooking time: About 45 minutes

Liquid hot pepper sauce and ground red pepper lend heat to these baked chicken wings. Serve with celery and sour cream–based blue cheese dip to help cool things off, if you wish.

- **4 pounds chicken wings, cut apart at joints**
  Red Hot Sauce (recipe follows)
  Blue Cheese Dip (recipe follows), optional
- **2 bunches celery (about 2 lbs. *total*), optional**

Discard wing tips or save for broth. Arrange chicken in 2 lightly greased 10- by 15-inch baking pans. Bake in a 400° oven until golden brown (about 30 minutes).

Meanwhile, prepare Red Hot Sauce. Remove pans from oven, drain off fat, and pour sauce over chicken, turning to coat well. Return pans to oven and continue baking, turning wings once or twice, until sauce is bubbling and edges of wings are crisp (about 15 more minutes).

Meanwhile, prepare Blue Cheese Dip and break celery stalks from head, if desired; remove leaves and set aside. Slice stalks lengthwise and place in a bowl.

Arrange chicken on a platter and garnish with reserved celery leaves, if used. Offer with celery stalks and cheese dip. Makes about 4 dozen appetizers.

Red Hot Sauce. Mix ½ cup *each* **vinegar** and **water,** ¼ cup **tomato paste,** 4 teaspoons **sugar,** 1 to 3 tablespoons (or to taste) **liquid hot pepper seasoning,** and 1 to 3 teaspoons (or to taste) **ground red pepper** (cayenne).

Per appetizer: 45 calories, 4 g protein, .8 g carbohydrates, 3 g total fat, 12 mg cholesterol, 39 mg sodium

Blue Cheese Dip. Coarsely mash ¼ pound **blue-veined cheese.** Stir in 1 cup **sour cream,** 1 teaspoon minced **garlic,** ½ teaspoon **dry mustard,** and ⅛ teaspoon **pepper.** If made ahead, cover and refrigerate for up to 3 days. Makes 1⅓ cups.

Per tablespoon: 43 calories, 2 g protein, .6 g carbohydrates, 4 g total fat, 9 mg cholesterol, 81 mg sodium

HOISIN CHICKEN WINGS

Preparation time: About 5 minutes
Marinating time: At least 1 hour
Cooking time: About 12 minutes

Take chicken drummettes, the meatiest portion of the wings, and marinate them in a bold blend of hoisin sauce, garlic, and sherry. Then quickly grill and watch them disappear.

- **⅓ cup hoisin sauce**
- **2 tablespoons dry sherry**
- **1 tablespoon lemon juice**
- **1 clove garlic, minced or pressed**
- **1½ pounds chicken drummettes (meatiest part of wing)**

Mix hoisin, sherry, lemon juice, and garlic. Add chicken, turning to coat. Cover and refrigerate for at least 1 hour or until next day.

Lift chicken from marinade, reserving marinade. Place on a greased grill 4 to 6 inches above a solid bed of medium coals. Cook, turning occasionally and brushing with marinade, until meat near bone is no longer pink when cut (about 12 minutes). Makes about 1½ dozen appetizers.

Per appetizer: 45 calories, 5 g protein, .8 g carbohydrates, 2 g total fat, 20 mg cholesterol, 98 mg sodium

CHICKEN YAKITORI

Preparation time: About 30 minutes
Marinating time: About 15 minutes
Cooking time: About 12 minutes

A simple marinade of soy sauce and sherry flavors chicken thighs and livers. Thread the meat on separate skewers to take into account their different cooking times.

- **½ cup soy sauce**
- **½ cup cream sherry, sake, or mirin**
- **3 tablespoons sugar**
- **6 large chicken thighs, skinned and boned**
- **½ pound chicken livers**
- **2 bunches green onions (including tops), cut into 1½-inch lengths**

Soak 16 short bamboo skewers in hot water to cover for 30 minutes.

Meanwhile, in a 1- to 1½-quart pan, boil soy, sherry, and sugar over high heat; reduce heat, cover, and simmer for 3 minutes. Pour into a shallow baking pan and set aside.

Cut thighs into bite-size pieces. Cut each liver in half. Thread thigh meat and livers on separate skewers, including several onion pieces on each. Marinate in soy mixture, turning once or twice, for 15 minutes.

Lift skewers from marinade, reserving marinade. Place on a lightly greased grill 4 to 6 inches above a solid bed of low coals. Cook, turning occasionally and brushing with marinade, until livers are firm but still moist in center when cut (about 5 minutes) and thigh meat is no longer pink in center when cut (about 8 minutes). Makes 16 appetizers.

Per appetizer: 69 calories, 9 g protein, 3 g carbohydrates, 2 g total fat, 89 mg cholesterol, 297 mg sodium

CHICKEN SATAY

Preparation time: About 20 minutes
Marinating time: At least 1½ hours
Cooking time: About 14 minutes

Dip broiled chicken chunks in a spicy peanut sauce for a Southeast Asian treat.

- 1 **clove garlic, minced or pressed**
- 2 **tablespoons soy sauce**
- 1 **tablespoon salad oil**
- 1 **teaspoon** *each* **ground cumin and ground coriander**
- 2 **whole chicken breasts (about 2 lbs.** *total***), split, skinned, and boned**
  Basting Sauce (recipe follows)
  Peanut Sauce (recipe follows)

Mix garlic, soy, oil, cumin, and coriander. Cut chicken into ¾-inch chunks. Add to marinade, stirring to coat evenly. Cover and refrigerate for at least 1½ hours or up to 2 hours.

Meanwhile, prepare Basting Sauce and Peanut Sauce; set aside. Also, soak 16 bamboo skewers in hot water to cover for 30 minutes.

Thread 4 or 5 cubes of chicken on each skewer. Place on a rack in a broiler pan; brush with half the baste. Broil 4 to 6 inches below heat, turning once and brushing with remaining baste, until no longer pink in center when cut (about 10 minutes).

Offer with sauce for dipping. Makes about 16 appetizers.

Basting Sauce. Mix 3 tablespoons **lemon juice,** 2 tablespoons **soy sauce,** and ¼ teaspoon *each* **ground cumin** and **ground coriander.**

Per appetizer: 94 calories, 17 g protein, 1 g carbohydrates, 2 g total fat, 43 mg cholesterol, 435 mg sodium

Peanut Sauce. In a 1- to 1½-quart pan, boil 1 cup **water,** ⅔ cup **creamy** or crunchy **peanut butter,** and 2 cloves **garlic,** minced or pressed, over medium-high heat, stirring, until

thickened (about 4 minutes). Remove from heat and stir in 2 tablespoons firmly packed **brown sugar,** 1½ tablespoons **lemon juice,** 1 tablespoon **soy sauce,** and ¼ to ½ teaspoon **crushed red pepper.** Let cool to room temperature. Makes 1½ cups.

Per tablespoon: 57 calories, 3 g protein, 3 g carbohydrates, 4 g total fat, 0 mg cholesterol, 93 mg sodium

CHUTNEY CHICKEN ROLLS

Preparation time: About 15 minutes
Cooking time: About 15 minutes

Nestled in the center of tender chicken rolls is a tempting mixture of almonds and chutney.

- 2 **tablespoons light rum**
- 3 **tablespoons butter or margarine, melted**
  About ⅓ cup fine dry seasoned bread crumbs
- 3 **whole chicken breasts (about 3 lbs.** *total***), split, skinned, and boned**
- 6 **tablespoons Major Grey's chutney, chopped**
- 2 **tablespoons slivered almonds**

Combine rum and butter in a shallow dish. Pour crumbs onto wax paper.

Place each breast half between sheets of plastic wrap. Pound with a flat-surfaced mallet until ¼ inch thick. Lay skinned sides down. Place 1 tablespoon of the chutney and 1 teaspoon of the almonds in center of each. Roll up to enclose, fastening with wooden picks. Dip in rum mixture and coat with crumbs. Place in a baking pan and drizzle with any remaining rum mixture.

Bake in a 425° oven until no longer pink in center when cut (about 15 minutes). Cut rolls in half. Makes 1 dozen appetizers.

Per appetizer: 147 calories, 18 g protein, 8 g carbohydrates, 5 g total fat, 51 mg cholesterol, 182 mg sodium

CHILI CHICKEN CHUNKS

Preparation time: About 30 minutes
Cooking time: About 15 minutes

Chunks of chicken breast are fried in a crunchy cornmeal crust until golden, ready for dipping into Guacamole (recipe on page 15).

- 3 **whole chicken breasts (about 3 lbs.** *total***), split, skinned, and boned**
- ¾ **cup all-purpose flour**
- ¼ **cup yellow cornmeal**
- 2 **teaspoons chili powder**
- ½ **teaspoon** *each* **paprika and salt**
- ¼ **teaspoon** *each* **ground cumin and dry oregano leaves**
- ⅛ **teaspoon pepper**
- ¾ **cup beer**
  Salad oil

Cut chicken into 1- to 1½-inch chunks; set aside. In a bowl, mix flour, cornmeal, chili powder, paprika, salt, cumin, oregano, and pepper. Add beer and stir until smooth. Add chicken, stirring to coat evenly.

In a deep 3- to 4-quart pan, heat about 1½ inches oil to 350°F on a deep-frying thermometer. Lift chicken from batter, a piece at a time, and add to pan (do not crowd). Cook, stirring occasionally, until browned and no longer pink in center when cut (about 2 minutes). Drain on paper towels.

If made ahead, cool, cover, and refrigerate until next day; to reheat, lay chicken in a paper towel–lined pan and place in a 350° oven until hot (about 15 minutes).

Offer with wooden picks. Makes about 8 dozen appetizers.

Per appetizer: 22 calories, 2 g protein, 1 g carbohydrates, .9 g total fat, 5 mg cholesterol, 18 mg sodium

Alternate chicken breasts with tropical fruits on bamboo skewers and broil quickly for Curried Chicken & Fruit Kebabs (recipe on facing page). You can use either papaya or kumquats with chunks of banana and pineapple.

Pictured on facing page
CURRIED CHICKEN & FRUIT KEBABS

Preparation time: About 25 minutes
Marinating time: At least 2 hours
Cooking time: About 12 minutes

Alternate tropical fruits with chunks of chicken breast on skewers. Your favorite oil and vinegar salad dressing enlivened by curry serves as a marinade.

3 whole chicken breasts (about 3 lbs. *total*), split, skinned, and boned
¾ cup bottled oil and vinegar salad dressing
2 teaspoons curry powder
3 medium-size green-tipped bananas
1 medium-size papaya or 20 preserved kumquats, drained
   About 2 cups fresh pineapple chunks
⅓ cup honey
   Lime wedges

Cut chicken into bite-size pieces (you should have at least 60). Mix salad dressing and curry powder; add chicken, stirring gently to coat. Cover and refrigerate for at least 2 hours or until next day.

Soak 20 bamboo skewers in hot water to cover for 30 minutes.

Shortly before cooking, peel bananas and cut into 1-inch slices; brush with marinade. Peel, halve, and seed papaya; cut into 1-inch cubes. Alternately thread chicken on skewers with 1 piece each pineapple, banana, and papaya. Stir honey into remaining marinade and brush over kebabs.

Broil 3 to 4 inches below heat, turning once and brushing with marinade, until chicken is no longer pink in center when cut (about 12 minutes). Offer with lime. Makes 20 appetizers.

Per appetizer: 138 calories, 11 g protein, 13 g carbohydrates, 5 g total fat, 26 mg cholesterol, 162 mg sodium

MUSSEL & CLAM APPETIZER

Preparation time: About 1 hour
Cooking time: About 30 minutes

A plate piled high with shelled mussels and clams invites guests to dig in! Red and green salsas top the shellfish served on toasted French bread.

1 cup Salsa Fresca (recipe on page 17)
1½ cups Tomatillo Salsa (recipe on page 17)
3 pounds mussels, scrubbed
1 cup *each* dry white wine and water
2 tablespoons lemon juice
1 pound clams (suitable for steaming), scrubbed
3 small French baguettes (8 oz. *each*), sliced ½ inch thick, lightly toasted
   Lime wedges

Prepare Salsa Fresca and Tomatillo Salsa; set aside.

Discard any mussels that don't close when tapped. Pull beard (clump of fibers along side of shell) off each mussel with a quick tug.

In a 6- to 8-quart pan, simmer mussels, wine, water, and lemon juice, covered, over medium-high heat just until shells open (about 5 minutes). Lift out with a slotted spoon, discarding any mussels that don't open. Let cool. Meanwhile, add clams, about a third at a time, to pan, cover, and simmer just until open (about 8 minutes). Lift out with a slotted spoon, discarding any clams that don't open. Let cool.

Remove mussels and clams from shells and pile in a large plate. Spoon shellfish onto bread slices; top with salsas and a squeeze of lime. Makes about 3 dozen appetizers.

Per appetizer: 83 calories, 5 g protein, 12 g carbohydrates, 1 g total fat, 9 mg cholesterol, 161 mg sodium

GARLIC MUSSELS ON THE HALF SHELL

Preparation time: About 30 minutes
Cooking time: About 10 minutes

Steamed mussels on the half shell are easy and elegant hors d'oeuvres. Freshly grated Parmesan cheese and garlic top the succulent shellfish.

1½ pounds mussels, scrubbed
1 cup dry white wine
¼ cup olive or salad oil
⅓ cup freshly grated Parmesan cheese
3 large cloves garlic, minced or pressed
1 tablespoon finely chopped parsley

Discard any mussels that don't close when tapped. Pull beard (clump of fibers along side of shell) off each mussel with a quick tug.

In a 5- to 6-quart pan, simmer mussels and wine, covered, over medium-high heat just until shells open (about 5 minutes). Lift out with a slotted spoon, discarding any mussels that don't open.

When mussels are cool enough to handle, remove meat from shells, discarding half of each shell. Arrange remaining half shells in a single layer in a heatproof serving dish. Place a mussel in each shell. In a small bowl, stir together oil, 3 tablespoons of the cheese, and garlic; drizzle mixture over mussels.

Broil 4 inches below heat just until cheese begins to melt and mussels are hot (about 5 minutes). Sprinkle with parsley and remaining cheese. Offer with wooden picks. Makes about 3 dozen appetizers.

Per appetizer: 23 calories, 1 g protein, .4 g carbohydrates, 2 g total fat, 2 mg cholesterol, 33 mg sodium

Succulent seafood, hearty beef balls, creamy cheese dip, spicy potato rounds: this symphony of starters cooks in no time. Your microwave lets you orchestrate a variety of delicious overtures to a meal in just minutes.

SIZZLING CURRIED SHRIMP

**Preparation time: About 15 minutes
Cooking time: 4½ to 6 minutes**

Shrimp absorb the flavor of a piquant butter sauce while cooking to moist perfection in the microwave.

¼ cup butter or margarine
1 large clove garlic, minced or pressed
1½ teaspoons curry powder
1 teaspoon mustard seeds, slightly crushed
½ teaspoon crushed dried hot red chiles
   Chives (optional)
1 pound medium-size raw shrimp (about 36 per lb.), shelled and deveined
2 teaspoons lemon juice
¼ cup chopped cilantro (coriander) or sliced green onions (including tops)
   Salt

Place butter in a 9- to 10-inch microwave-safe baking dish. Microwave, uncovered, on **HIGH (100%)** for 1 to 1½ minutes or until melted.

Stir in garlic, curry powder, mustard seeds, and chiles. Microwave, uncovered, on **HIGH (100%)** for 30 more seconds.

Wrap and tie a chive around each shrimp, if desired. Add shrimp to dish and microwave, uncovered, on

MICROWAVE MEDLEY

HIGH (100%) for 3 to 4 minutes, stirring once or twice, or just until shrimp are bright pink. Stir in lemon juice and cilantro, and season to taste with salt. Offer with wooden picks. Makes about 3 dozen appetizers.

Per appetizer: 23 calories, 2 g protein, .2 g carbohydrates, 1 g total fat, 19 mg cholesterol, 28 mg sodium

ONIONS IN BASIL-PARMESAN BUTTER

**Preparation time: About 10 minutes
Cooking time: 11 to 14 minutes**

Tiny frozen onions cook quickly in the microwave. Toss them in basil-accented butter and serve them tucked into pocket bread wedges.

1 package (10 oz.) frozen small whole onions
2 tablespoons butter or margarine
¼ cup slivered fresh basil leaves or 1 tablespoon dry basil leaves
¼ cup grated Parmesan cheese
   Salt and pepper
5 or 6 pocket breads (6-in. diameter), cut into quarters

Place frozen onions in a shallow 9-inch microwave-safe dish. Dot with butter and sprinkle with basil. Microwave, uncovered, on **HIGH (100%)** for 8 to 10 minutes, stirring once or twice, or until onions are tender when pierced. Sprinkle with cheese and season to taste with salt and pepper.

If desired, microwave pocket bread quarters, 4 at a time, on **HIGH (100%)** for about 30 seconds or just until warm.

Spoon 2 or 3 onions and a little sauce into pocket bread wedges. Makes 20 to 24 appetizers.

Per appetizer: 62 calories, 2 g protein, 10 g carbohydrates, 1 g total fat, 4 mg cholesterol, 120 mg sodium

ZESTY BARBECUED MEATBALLS

**Preparation time: About 15 minutes
Cooking time: 8 to 10 minutes**

Choose your favorite barbecue sauce—from hickory-smoked to super-hot—for these meaty morsels, always popular party fare.

1 egg, lightly beaten
1 tablespoon Worcestershire
¼ cup *each* fine dry bread crumbs and thinly sliced green onions (including tops)
1 pound lean ground beef
½ cup prepared barbecue sauce

Mix egg, Worcestershire, bread crumbs, and onions. Add ground beef, mixing until well combined. Shape into 1-inch balls (you should have about 36). Arrange in a single layer in a microwave-safe 7- by 11-inch or 8-inch square dish.

Cover and microwave on **HIGH (100%)** for 5 minutes. Spoon off and discard drippings; rearrange meatballs, if necessary, so that uncooked ones are at outside of dish. Drizzle with barbecue sauce. Microwave, uncovered, on **HIGH (100%)** for 3 to 5 more minutes or until meatballs are no longer pink in center when cut. Stir gently to coat with sauce.

Offer with wooden picks. Makes about 3 dozen appetizers.

Per appetizer: 33 calories, 3 g protein, 1 g carbohydrates, 2 g total fat, 13 mg cholesterol, 45 mg sodium

HAM & PINEAPPLE PUPUS

Preparation time: About 15 minutes
Cooking time: 4½ to 6 minutes

Fresh pineapple takes these Hawaiian-inspired treats out of the ordinary. Substitute juicy pears for the pineapple for equally satisfying results.

¼ **pound thinly sliced baked ham**
   About 3 dozen 1-inch cubes fresh pineapple
¼ **cup catsup**
1 **teaspoon dry mustard**
2 **tablespoons soy sauce**
1 **tablespoon brown sugar**
1 **small clove garlic, minced or pressed**

Cut ham into 1-inch-wide strips. Wrap a strip around each pineapple cube, spearing with a wooden pick to secure.

In a small bowl, mix catsup, mustard, soy, sugar, and garlic. Drizzle a little of the sauce over each pupu, reserving remaining sauce.

Arrange pupus, about a dozen at a time, on a flat 9- to 10-inch microwave-safe plate. Microwave, uncovered, on **HIGH (100%)** for 1½ to 2 minutes, rotating plate a half-turn midway through cooking, or until ham is sizzling and pineapple is heated through.

Offer with remaining sauce for dipping. Makes about 3 dozen appetizers.

Per appetizer: 16 calories, .8 g protein, 2 g carbohydrates, .3 g total fat, 2 mg cholesterol, 124 mg sodium

Ham & Pear Pupus

Follow directions for **Ham & Pineapple Pupus,** but omit pineapple. Core 2 medium-size firm-ripe **pears** and cut each into 8 wedges; cut each wedge in half. Wrap a strip of ham around each half-wedge and continue as directed. Makes 32 appetizers.

Per appetizer: 17 calories, .9 g protein, 3 g carbohydrates, .4 g total fat, 2 mg cholesterol, 140 mg sodium

JALAPEÑO & BACON POTATOES

Preparation time: About 10 minutes
Cooking time: 13½ to 19 minutes

Melted jalapeño-flavored cheese and a sprinkling of bacon top tender potato rounds in this easily made hot hors d'oeuvre.

1 **pound small red thin-skinned potatoes (2-in. diameter), scrubbed**
4 **slices bacon**
1 **cup (4 oz.) lightly packed shredded jalapeño jack cheese**

Pierce each potato in several places with a fork. Arrange in a circle in a microwave oven. Microwave, uncovered, on **HIGH (100%)** for 6 to 8 minutes, rotating potatoes once, or until potatoes are tender when pierced. Let cool briefly.

Slice potatoes about ¼ inch thick. Arrange slices in a single layer on 2 flat 10-inch microwave-safe plates. Set aside.

Place bacon on several thicknesses of paper towels in a 7- by 11-inch microwave-safe baking dish or on a microwave-safe broiling rack; cover with a paper towel. Microwave on **HIGH (100%)** for 3½ to 6 minutes or until bacon is browned. Let cool briefly; then coarsely crush.

Place a rounded teaspoon of the cheese on each potato slice. Sprinkle with bacon. Microwave, uncovered, a plateful at a time, on **HIGH (100%)** for 2 to 2½ minutes or until cheese is melted and bubbling. Makes 3 to 3½ dozen appetizers.

Per appetizer: 24 calories, 1 g protein, 2 g carbohydrates, 1 g total fat, 4 mg cholesterol, 31 mg sodium

NEOCLASSIC CHEESE FONDUE

Preparation time: About 15 minutes
Cooking time: 5 to 10 minutes

Because it's made in the microwave, this version of Swiss fondue takes little time and attention.

1 **cup (4 oz.) *each* shredded aged Swiss (Emmenthaler) and Gruyère cheese**
2 **teaspoons cornstarch**
½ **teaspoon dry mustard**
¾ **cup dry white wine**
1 **tablespoon kirsch (optional)**
   Freshly grated nutmeg
   About 4 cups ½-inch cubes firm French bread

Lightly mix Swiss, Gruyère, cornstarch, and mustard; set aside.

Pour wine into a deep 1½- to 2-quart microwave-safe casserole. Microwave, uncovered, on **HIGH (100%)** for 2 to 5 minutes or just until wine begins to bubble. Remove from oven. Add cheese mixture, a handful at a time, stirring after each addition, until cheese is soft. Return to oven and microwave on **MEDIUM (50%)** for 3 to 5 minutes, stirring once or twice, or until fondue is thick and bubbly. Stir well. Blend in kirsch, if desired, and sprinkle with nutmeg.

Keep warm on an electric warming tray or over a candle warmer. Offer with bread cubes for dipping. Makes about 6 servings.

Per serving: 231 calories, 13 g protein, 16 g carbohydrates, 12 g total fat, 39 mg cholesterol, 269 mg sodium

Pictured on facing page

SAUTÉED SQUID & SHIITAKE MUSHROOMS

Preparation time: About 20 minutes, plus 30 minutes to soak dried mushrooms
Cooking time: About 15 minutes

Quickly cook rings of squid and serve with shiitake mushrooms in a wine-enriched cream sauce on toast rounds. For an elegant presentation, garnish with raspberries, lemon peel, and mint.

1 **pound cleaned squid tubes (mantles)**
5 **large fresh or dried shiitake mushrooms** (*each* 2- to 3-in. diameter)
2 **tablespoons olive oil**
1 **cup** *each* **dry white wine and whipping cream**
3 **tablespoons raspberry vinegar or lemon juice**
½ **teaspoon freshly ground pepper Salt**
30 **slices cocktail rye bread, lightly toasted**
Raspberries (optional)
Long, thin shreds of lemon peel (optional)
Mint sprigs (optional)

Cut squid tubes crosswise into ⅛- to ¼-inch-thick rings; set aside.

If using dried mushrooms, soak in warm water to cover until pliable (about 30 minutes); drain. Cut off and discard stems of fresh or dried mushrooms; slice caps thinly.

Heat oil in a wide frying pan over medium heat. Add mushrooms and cook, stirring, until soft (about 3 minutes). Lift out and set aside.

Add wine and cream to pan. Bring to a boil; reduce heat, add squid, and adjust heat so mixture barely simmers. Cook, stirring occasionally, until squid is tender (about 5 minutes). With a slotted spoon, lift out squid and add to mushrooms.

Increase heat to high and boil liquid in pan, stirring occasionally, until reduced to 1 cup (about 4 minutes). Return squid and mushrooms to pan; then remove from heat. Stir in vinegar and pepper; season to taste with salt.

Evenly spoon squid mixture onto toast slices. Garnish with raspberries, lemon peel, and mint, if desired. Makes 2½ dozen appetizers.

Per appetizer: 65 calories, 3 g protein, 5 g carbohydrates, 4 g total fat, 44 mg cholesterol, 49 mg sodium

HAWAII SCALLOP SKEWERS

Preparation time: About 25 minutes
Marinating time: At least 2 hours
Cooking time: About 8 minutes

Before you put on the steaks, quickly grill these colorful skewers of scallops, mushrooms, bacon, and bell peppers for a delicious meal opener. The soy marinade doubles as the basting sauce.

16 **scallops (1¼ to 1½ lbs.** *total*)
Soy Marinade (recipe follows)
16 **medium-size to large mushrooms (about 1 lb.** *total*)
4 **slices bacon**
2 **small red bell peppers, seeded and cut into 1½-inch squares**

Rinse scallops and pat dry.

Prepare Soy Marinade and pour into a deep bowl; add scallops and mushrooms and turn to coat. Cover and refrigerate for at least 2 hours or up to 4 hours, turning several times. Meanwhile, soak 8 bamboo skewers in hot water to cover for 30 minutes.

In a wide frying pan, cook bacon over medium heat until partially cooked but still limp (about 3 minutes). Lift out and drain. Cut each slice into 4 pieces.

Lift scallops and mushrooms from marinade and drain briefly, reserving marinade. Thread scallops, mushrooms, bacon, and bell peppers alternately on skewers. Place on a well-greased grill 4 to 6 inches above a solid bed of hot coals. Cook, turning occasionally and brushing with marinade, until scallops are opaque inside when cut (about 5 minutes). Makes 8 appetizers.

Soy Marinade. Stir together ¼ cup **soy sauce;** 1 tablespoon *each* **lemon juice, dry sherry,** and **salad oil;** 2 cloves **garlic,** minced or pressed; and 1 teaspoon *each* **sugar** and minced **fresh ginger.**

Per appetizer: 117 calories, 16 g protein, 6 g carbohydrates, 3 g total fat, 29 mg cholesterol, 447 mg sodium

SHRIMP IN MINT LEAVES

Preparation time: About 35 minutes
Cooking time: About 4 minutes

Fresh mint leaves wrap and flavor shrimp coated with lemon and butter. Quickly barbecued, the succulent morsels are delicious hot off the grill.

24 **medium-size raw shrimp (about ⅔ lb.** *total*), **shelled and deveined**
3 **tablespoons lemon juice**
¼ **cup butter or margarine, melted**
24 **large fresh mint leaves**

Soak 12 bamboo skewers in hot water to cover for 30 minutes. Meanwhile, mix shrimp, lemon juice, and butter. Fold a mint leaf around each shrimp. Thread 2 shrimp closely together on each skewer. Brush with any remaining butter mixture.

Place shrimp on a greased grill 2 to 4 inches above a solid bed of hot coals. Cook, turning once, until shrimp are opaque when cut (about 4 minutes). Makes 1 dozen appetizers.

Per appetizer: 28 calories, 2 g protein, .2 g carbohydrates, 2 g total fat, 21 mg cholesterol, 35 mg sodium

Dress up your next dinner party with this elegant hors d'oeuvre, Sautéed Squid & Shiitake Mushrooms (recipe on facing page). The creamy canapé is served on rye rounds and garnished with fresh raspberries.

COCONUT SHRIMP

Preparation time: About 25 minutes
Marinating time: At least 30 minutes
Cooking time: About 10 minutes

Crisp shredded coconut coats butter-flied shrimp sizzled in hot oil. Look for coconut milk and panko (Japanese-style coarse bread crumbs) in Asian or other well-stocked supermarkets.

- 12 colossal-size shrimp (about 15 per lb.), shelled (leave tails on, if desired) and deveined
- 1 tablespoon dry sherry
- ⅛ teaspoon curry powder
- ¾ cup all-purpose flour
- 2 teaspoons cornstarch
- ½ teaspoon baking powder
- ½ cup canned or thawed frozen coconut milk; or ½ cup milk and ½ teaspoon coconut extract
- 2 to 3 tablespoons water
- 1½ cups sweetened shredded dry coconut
- ¾ cup panko or coarse fresh bread crumbs
  Salad oil
  Salt and pepper
  Mango chutney (optional)

Cut a slit almost completely through back of each shrimp. Mix sherry, curry powder, and shrimp. Cover and refrigerate for at least 30 minutes or until next day.

In a bowl, mix ½ cup of the flour, cornstarch, and baking powder. Stir in coconut milk and enough of the water to make a smooth, thin batter.

On wax paper, mix shredded coconut and panko. Put remaining ¼ cup flour on another piece of wax paper.

In a deep 3- to 4-quart pan, heat about 1½ inches oil to 350°F on a deep-frying thermometer. Laying shrimp flat, coat with flour, batter, and then panko mixture. Cook shrimp, 3 or 4 at a time, turning occasionally, until golden (about 1½ minutes). Skim oil often to remove browned bits. Drain on paper towels. Season to taste with salt and pepper.

Offer with chutney for dipping, if desired. Makes 1 dozen appetizers.

Per appetizer: 147 calories, 7 g protein, 13 g carbohydrates, 8 g total fat, 37 mg cholesterol, 93 mg sodium

PHOENIX-TAIL SHRIMP

Preparation time: About 30 minutes
Cooking time: About 25 minutes

Coated with a crunchy puff of batter, these deep-fried shrimp are ready for dipping in hot mustard or a sauce of your choice.

- 1 cup all-purpose flour
- 2½ teaspoons baking powder
- ¼ teaspoon salt
  Dash of ground white pepper
- 1 cup water
  Salad oil
- 1 pound medium-size raw shrimp (about 36 per lb.), shelled (leave tails on) and deveined
  Hot mustard (optional)

Combine flour, baking powder, salt, and pepper. Add water and stir until batter is smooth.

In a deep 3- to 4-quart pan, heat about 1½ inches oil to 350°F on a deep-frying thermometer. Holding shrimp by tail, dip into batter (do not dip tail) and cook, 3 or 4 at a time, turning occasionally, until golden (about 1¼ minutes). Drain on paper towels.

Offer with hot mustard for dipping, if desired. Makes about 3 dozen appetizers.

Per appetizer: 34 calories, 2 g protein, 3 g carbohydrates, 1 g total fat, 16 mg cholesterol, 60 mg sodium

CHEESE-FILLED SHRIMP

Preparation time: About 45 minutes
Cooking time: About 10 minutes

Plump shrimp are stuffed with cheese, wrapped with bacon, and deep-fried until golden for an impressive treat.

- 12 colossal-size raw shrimp (about 15 per lb.), shelled (leave tails on, if desired) and deveined
- 2 ounces jack cheese
- 6 slices bacon, cut in half crosswise
  About ⅓ cup fine dry bread crumbs
  Salad oil
  Tomato-based cocktail sauce (optional)

Starting about ¼ inch from head end, cut along back of each shrimp to make a pocket about ¾ inch deep and 1½ inches long. In center of slit, make a ¼-inch cut through shrimp.

Cut cheese into twelve 1-inch triangles about ½ inch thick. Tuck a point of each cheese triangle into ¼-inch cut in each shrimp. Tightly wrap a half-slice of bacon around shrimp. Impale a slender wooden skewer through tail end of shrimp and then through bacon and cheese. (At this point, you may cover and refrigerate until next day.)

Place bread crumbs on wax paper. Coat shrimp with crumbs. In a deep 3- to 4-quart pan, heat about 1½ inches oil to 350°F on a deep-frying thermometer. Cook shrimp, 3 or 4 at a time, turning occasionally, until cheese begins to melt (about 1½ minutes). Drain on paper towels.

Offer with cocktail sauce for dipping, if desired. Makes 1 dozen appetizers.

Per appetizer: 93 calories, 7 g protein, 2 g carbohydrates, 6 g total fat, 44 mg cholesterol, 133 mg sodium

SHRIMP ON CABBAGE SQUARES

Preparation time: About 40 minutes
Cooking time: About 8 minutes

Begin an Asian-inspired banquet with your own dim sum. Shrimp paste sparked with ginger and garlic steams on bite-size squares of napa cabbage.

Fresh Shrimp Paste (recipe follows)
10 **to 12 large napa cabbage leaves**
48 **julienne strips thinly sliced cooked ham (*each* about 1 in. long)**
24 **cilantro (coriander) leaves Soy sauce (optional)**

Prepare Fresh Shrimp Paste; set aside.

Cut off leafy portions of cabbage; cut stems into twenty-four 1½-inch squares. Reserve leaves and trimmings for other uses.

In a wok or deep, wide pan, arrange cabbage squares on a rack over about 1 inch boiling water. Cover and steam over high heat just until cabbage is slightly wilted (about 2 minutes). Drain well.

On each cabbage square, mound about 1½ teaspoons of the shrimp paste. Lightly press 2 ham strips and a cilantro leaf into shrimp paste. Place cabbage squares, slightly apart, on an 11- to 12-inch heatproof plate; cover with plastic wrap. (At this point, you may refrigerate for up to 8 hours.)

Place plate on a rack over 1 inch boiling water in wok. Cover and steam over high heat just until shrimp paste feels firm when lightly pressed (about 6 minutes). Offer with soy for dipping, if desired. Makes 2 dozen appetizers.

Fresh Shrimp Paste. Shell and devein ½ pound medium-size **raw shrimp** (about 36 per lb.). In a food processor, combine shrimp; 2 **egg whites;** 1 tablespoon *each* **dry sherry** and minced **fresh ginger;** 1 clove **garlic,** minced or pressed; 2 teaspoons **cornstarch;** 1 teaspoon **sugar;** ½ teaspoon *each* **salt** and **sesame oil;** and ⅛ teaspoon **ground white pepper.** Whirl until mixture forms a smooth paste. (Or finely mince shrimp with a knife; then combine with remaining ingredients and beat until well blended and sticky.)

Per appetizer: 18 calories, 2 g protein, 1 g carbohydrates, .4 g total fat, 13 mg cholesterol, 90 mg sodium

BARBECUED SHRIMP

Preparation time: About 15 minutes
Marinating time: At least 4 hours
Cooking time: About 4 minutes

Marinate shrimp in a sweet-sour sauce and then either grill or broil them for a speedy appetizer offering.

1 **can (8 oz.) tomato sauce**
½ **cup molasses**
1 **teaspoon dry mustard Dash of liquid hot pepper seasoning**
¼ **cup salad oil**
⅛ **teaspoon dry thyme leaves Salt and pepper**
2 **pounds medium-size raw shrimp (about 36 per lb.), shelled and deveined**

Mix tomato sauce, molasses, mustard, hot pepper seasoning, oil, and thyme until well blended. Season to taste with salt and pepper. Add shrimp, turning to coat. Cover and refrigerate for at least 4 hours or until next day.

Soak bamboo skewers in hot water to cover for 30 minutes. Lift out shrimp, reserving marinade, and thread on skewers. Place on a greased grill 6 inches above a solid bed of low-glowing coals. (Or place

on a rimmed baking sheet and broil about 6 inches below heat.) Cook, brushing frequently with marinade and turning once, until shrimp are opaque when cut (about 4 minutes). Makes about 6 dozen appetizers.

Per appetizer: 24 calories, 2 g protein, 2 g carbohydrates, .9 g total fat, 16 mg cholesterol, 35 mg sodium

Pictured on page 30
BAKED SHRIMP WITH GARLIC

Preparation time: About 15 minutes
Marinating time: At least 4 hours
Cooking time: About 10 minutes

With just five ingredients and some advance preparation, you can produce a delicious hot appetizer in minutes. Simply pop the marinated shrimp in the oven when your guests arrive.

½ **cup olive oil**
1 **clove garlic, minced or pressed**
¼ **teaspoon salt**
1 **pound medium-size raw shrimp (about 36 per lb.), shelled and deveined**
1 **tablespoon finely minced parsley Parsley sprigs (optional)**

Mix oil, garlic, and salt. Add shrimp, turning to coat; sprinkle with minced parsley. Cover and refrigerate for at least 4 hours or until next day.

Transfer to a 10- by 15-inch baking pan. Bake in a 375° oven until shrimp are opaque when cut (about 10 minutes). Arrange in a bowl. Garnish with parsley sprigs, if desired. Offer with wooden picks. Makes about 3 dozen appetizers.

Per appetizer: 37 calories, 2 g protein, .1 g carbohydrates, 3 g total fat, 16 mg cholesterol, 30 mg sodium

Your company will think you've fussed for hours, but
Mint Sauce (recipe on page 10) offered with pea pods,
Meatballs Wrapped in Basil Leaves (recipe on page 49),
and Eggplant & Goat Cheese Rolls (recipe on facing page)
are quick to prepare.

Pictured on facing page

EGGPLANT & GOAT CHEESE ROLLS

◆

**Preparation time: About 15 minutes
Cooking time: About 13 minutes**

Crisp watercress and tangy goat cheese are paired in an intriguing eggplant roll. Use Oriental eggplants, if you can find them; they're usually sweeter and have smaller seeds than the regular kind.

- **1 pound Oriental eggplants (about 4 *total*) or regular eggplant, stems removed**
- **1½ tablespoons olive oil**
- **3 ounces soft goat cheese, such as Montrachet**
- **12 to 16 watercress sprigs, washed and dried**

Cut eggplants lengthwise into ¼- to ⅓-inch-thick slices (if using regular variety, cut slices in half lengthwise). Brush both sides with oil and place in a single layer in large baking pans. Bake in a 450° oven for 8 minutes; turn and continue baking until very soft when pressed (about 5 more minutes). Remove from pans and let cool.

Place about ½ teaspoon of the cheese at an end of each eggplant slice; top with a sprig of watercress, letting leaves overhang edges. Roll up. Makes 12 to 16 appetizers.

Per appetizer: 43 calories, 1 g protein, 2 g carbohydrates, 3 g total fat, 6 mg cholesterol, 39 mg sodium

MEXICAN BARBECUED CORN

◆

**Preparation time: About 5 minutes
Cooking time: About 8 minutes**

Corn coblets are a wonderful introduction to a summer barbecue. Season the corn with chili and lime juice or with garlic, basil, and Parmesan.

- **2 tablespoons salt**
- **1 teaspoon *each* chili powder and ground cumin**
- **4 medium-size ears corn, *each* cut into 3 chunks**
- **¼ cup salad oil**
- **2 limes, cut into wedges**

Mix salt, chili powder, and cumin; set aside.

Brush corn lightly with oil. Place on a lightly greased grill 4 to 6 inches above a solid bed of medium coals. Cook, turning occasionally, until kernels are lightly browned in several areas (about 8 minutes).

Offer with lime and salt mixture. Makes 1 dozen appetizers.

Per appetizer: 50 calories, 1 g protein, 7 g carbohydrates, 3 g total fat, 0 mg cholesterol, 1,105 mg sodium

Barbecued Corn with Basil Butter

Prepare and barbecue corn as directed for **Mexican Barbecued Corn,** but omit salt, chili powder, cumin, and limes.

Meanwhile, in a 1-quart pan, combine ½ cup (¼ lb.) **butter** or margarine; 1 clove **garlic,** minced or pressed; and 2 tablespoons chopped **fresh basil leaves** or 1 tablespoon dry basil leaves. Place on grill slightly away from coals and heat, stirring occasionally, until butter is melted. Place about ½ cup **grated Parmesan cheese** in a bowl.

Offer corn with butter mixture and cheese.

Per appetizer: 110 calories, 2 g protein, 6 g carbohydrates, 9 g total fat, 23 mg cholesterol, 145 mg sodium

Pictured on page 46

ARTICHOKE HEARTS WITH BLUE CHEESE

◆

**Preparation time: About 30 minutes
Cooking time: About 20 minutes**

Guests will enjoy these tiny artichoke halves topped with blue cheese.

- **2 quarts water**
- **2 tablespoons lemon juice or vinegar**
- **12 small artichokes (*each* 2 in.-diameter) or 2 packages (10 oz. *each*) frozen artichoke hearts, thawed**
- **¼ cup butter or margarine, at room temperature**
- **3 ounces blue-veined cheese Lemon slices (optional)**

Combine water and lemon juice in a 5- to 6-quart pan. Remove and discard coarse outer leaves of fresh artichokes down to tender, pale yellow ones. Snip off thorny tips; trim stems to about ½ inch. (Or use 24 frozen artichoke halves.) As artichokes are trimmed, drop into water.

Bring water to a boil over high heat; reduce heat, cover, and simmer until artichoke bottoms are tender when pierced (about 10 minutes for either fresh or frozen artichokes). Drain; let cool. Cut whole artichokes in half lengthwise.

Arrange artichokes, cut sides up, in a baking pan. In a small bowl, mash butter and cheese until combined. Evenly spoon into artichokes. (At this point, you may cover and refrigerate until next day.)

Bake, uncovered, in a 350° oven just until cheese is melted (about 10 minutes). Garnish with lemon, if desired. Makes 2 dozen appetizers.

Per appetizer: 38 calories, 1 g protein, 2 g carbohydrates, 3 g total fat, 8 mg cholesterol, 80 mg sodium

Pictured on page 51

GARLIC-BUTTERED MUSHROOMS

◆

Preparation time: About 15 minutes
Cooking time: About 5 minutes

Freshly grated Parmesan adds extra flavor to a shallot- and parsley-enriched garlic butter that fills grilled mushroom caps.

Serve with thin slices of French bread to soak up the buttery juices.

⅓ cup butter or margarine, at room temperature
1 small shallot, finely chopped
2 cloves garlic, minced or pressed
2 tablespoons *each* finely chopped parsley and freshly grated Parmesan cheese
⅛ teaspoon ground white pepper
12 large mushrooms (about 1½ lbs. *total*)
1 small French baguette (8 oz.), sliced ½ inch thick

Mix butter, shallot, garlic, parsley, cheese, and pepper until well blended.

Twist off mushroom stems; reserve for other uses. Evenly spoon butter mixture into mushroom caps.

In a barbecue with a lid, place mushrooms, butter sides up, on a lightly greased grill 4 to 6 inches above a solid bed of medium coals. Cover barbecue and open dampers. (Or place mushrooms on a rack in a broiler pan and broil about 6 inches below heat.) Cook until butter is melted and mushrooms begin to shrivel slightly (about 5 minutes). Offer with bread to absorb buttery juices. Makes 1 dozen appetizers.

Per appetizer: 119 calories, 3 g protein, 13 g carbohydrates, 6 g total fat, 15 mg cholesterol, 179 mg sodium

MISO GRILLED MUSHROOMS

◆

Preparation time: About 15 minutes
Marinating time: At least 6 hours
Cooking time: About 5 minutes

Simply spear these hot mushrooms and dip them in a marinade made with sake, fresh ginger, and miso, a fermented soybean paste.

3 tablespoons miso
¼ cup sake or dry sherry
1 teaspoon grated fresh ginger
2 teaspoons honey
2 tablespoons lemon juice
2 tablespoons rice vinegar or distilled white vinegar
16 medium-size to large mushrooms (about 1 lb. *total*)
1 green onion (including top), thinly sliced

Mix miso, sake, ginger, honey, lemon juice, and vinegar until blended. Add mushrooms, stirring to coat. Cover and refrigerate for at least 6 hours or until next day.

Soak 8 bamboo skewers in hot water to cover for 30 minutes. Drain marinade into a small pan and set aside. Thread 2 mushrooms on each skewer and place on a lightly greased grill 4 to 6 inches above a solid bed of low-glowing coals. (Or place on a rack in a broiler pan and broil about 6 inches below heat.) Cook, brushing occasionally with marinade and turning once or twice, until browned (about 5 minutes).

Remove mushrooms from skewers. Heat remaining marinade, pour into a small bowl, and top with onion. Offer mushrooms with wooden picks. Makes 16 appetizers.

Per appetizer: 19 calories, 1 g protein, 4 g carbohydrates, .3 g total fat, 0 mg cholesterol, 119 mg sodium

HEAVENLY MUSHROOMS

◆

Preparation time: About 20 minutes
Cooking time: About 15 minutes

A touch of black lumpfish caviar elevates these mushrooms out of the ordinary. Red onion and parsley add color to the dill-flavored cream cheese filling. Serve with your favorite Champagne or sparkling mineral water with a twist of lemon.

20 medium-size to large mushrooms (about 1¼ lbs. *total*)
¼ cup butter or margarine, melted
2 tablespoons black lumpfish caviar
1 large package (8 oz.) cream cheese, at room temperature
2 teaspoons fresh dill or 1 teaspoon dill weed
2 tablespoons minced red or white onion
⅓ cup minced parsley

Twist off mushroom stems; reserve for other uses. Pour butter into a 9- by 13-inch baking pan. Add mushrooms, turning to coat, and arrange in pan, cavity sides up.

Rinse caviar in a fine strainer under cold running water until water runs clear; let drain.

Beat cheese, dill, and onion until blended; stir in caviar. Evenly mound cheese mixture in mushroom caps. (At this point, you may cover and refrigerate until next day.)

Bake, uncovered, in a 350° oven until cheese mixture is lightly browned (about 15 minutes). Evenly sprinkle mushrooms with parsley. Makes 20 appetizers.

Per appetizer: 72 calories, 2 g protein, 2 g carbohydrates, 7 g total fat, 28 mg cholesterol, 83 mg sodium

Pictured on page 30

FLORENTINE MUSHROOMS

◆

Preparation time: About 20 minutes
Cooking time: About 25 minutes

Mildly flavored Italian sausage mixed with spinach and two kinds of cheese—jack and ricotta—makes a hearty filling for mushroom caps.

¾ **pound mild Italian sausage, casing removed**
1 **pound spinach, stems removed, washed and dried**
1½ **tablespoons chopped fresh dill or 1 teaspoon dill weed**
1½ **cups (6 oz.) shredded jack cheese**
½ **cup ricotta cheese**
24 **medium-size to large mushrooms (about 1½ lbs. *total*)**
¼ **cup butter or margarine, melted**
   Dill sprigs (optional)

Crumble sausage into a wide frying pan over medium heat and cook, stirring occasionally, until no longer pink (about 7 minutes). With a slotted spoon, transfer to a bowl. Spoon off and discard all but 1 tablespoon of the drippings, reserving in pan.

Chop spinach leaves coarsely. Add to pan, cover, and cook until soft (about 1 minute). Drain well, pressing out moisture. Add to sausage; then lightly mix in chopped dill, jack, and ricotta.

Twist off mushroom stems; reserve for other uses. Pour butter into a 9- by 13-inch baking dish. Add mushrooms, turning to coat, and arrange in dish, cavity sides up. Evenly mound sausage mixture in caps. Bake in a 400° oven until hot (about 15 minutes).

Arrange on a platter. Garnish with dill sprigs, if desired. Makes 2 dozen appetizers.

Per appetizer: 98 calories, 5 g protein, 2 g carbohydrates, 8 g total fat, 21 mg cholesterol, 174 mg sodium

SHRIMP-STUFFED MUSHROOMS

◆

Preparation time: About 10 minutes
Cooking time: About 20 minutes

Succulent mushroom caps hold a delicate shrimp filling accented with crunchy water chestnuts. You can steam this Asian-inspired appetizer in a wok or large frying pan.

16 **medium-size to large mushrooms (about 1 lb. *total*)**
½ **teaspoon *each* salt and sugar**
1 **tablespoon soy sauce**
1 **cup regular-strength chicken broth**
   Shrimp Filling (recipe follows)
   Parsley sprigs
1 **jar (2 oz.) sliced pimentos, drained (optional)**

Twist off mushroom stems; reserve for other uses. In a 1- to 1½-quart pan, bring mushroom caps, salt, sugar, soy, and broth to a boil over medium-high heat. Reduce heat and simmer for 10 minutes.

Meanwhile, prepare Shrimp Filling; set aside.

Remove mushrooms from broth; drain and let cool slightly. Evenly mound filling in mushroom caps. Arrange, cavity sides up, on 1 or 2 serving plates that will fit inside a wok or wide frying pan. (At this point, you may cover and refrigerate for up to 8 hours; bring to room temperature before steaming.)

Place plate on a rack in wok or pan over 1½ to 2 inches boiling water. Cover and steam until filling is cooked through (about 10 minutes). Garnish with parsley and, if desired, pimentos. Makes 16 appetizers.

Shrimp Filling. Beat 1 **egg white** until foamy. Blend 2 teaspoons *each* **dry sherry** and **cornstarch;** stir into egg white along with ½ teaspoon *each* **salt** and grated **fresh ginger.** Add ¼ cup finely chopped **water chestnuts**

and ½ pound **raw shrimp,** shelled, deveined, and finely chopped. Mix until blended.

Per appetizer: 27 calories, 3 g protein, 3 g carbohydrates, .4 g total fat, 18 mg cholesterol, 285 mg sodium

CRISP-FRIED ONIONS

◆

Preparation time: About 20 minutes
Cooking time: About 25 minutes

These delicate, golden onion rings will disappear as soon as they're served, making everyone eager for more.

2 **large onions (about 1 lb. *total*)**
½ **cup all-purpose flour**
   Salad oil
   Salt

Peel and thinly slice onions; separate into rings. Place flour in a bag, add onions, and shake to coat evenly.

In a deep 3- to 4-quart pan, heat about 1½ inches oil to 300°F on a deep-frying thermometer. Add onions, about a quarter at a time, and cook, stirring often, until golden (about 5 minutes). Oil temperature will drop at first and then rise as onions brown; regulate heat accordingly.

With a slotted spoon, lift out onions and drain on paper towels (discard any scorched bits).

If made ahead, let cool completely, package airtight, and refrigerate for up to 3 days; to reheat, spread in a single layer in a shallow pan and place in a 350° oven until hot (about 2 minutes).

Pile in a napkin-lined basket or on a plate; season to taste with salt. Makes about 8 servings.

Per serving: 93 calories, 1 g protein, 10 g carbohydrates, 5 g total fat, 0 mg cholesterol, 1 mg sodium

GLAZED ONIONS WITH CORN, PEPPERS & SHRIMP

◆

Preparation time: About 10 minutes
Cooking time: About 15 minutes

Balsamic vinegar provides a rich-tasting glaze for onions, corn, and roasted peppers. Top the vegetable mélange with tiny shrimp and green onions, and serve with baguette slices.

- 3 tablespoons olive oil
- 1 package (10 oz.) frozen tiny whole onions
- 1 cup whole-kernel corn, fresh or frozen
- 3 tablespoons balsamic or red wine vinegar
- 1 teaspoon sugar
- 1 jar (7 oz.) roasted peppers, drained and cut into ½-inch slivers
- ¼ pound small cooked shrimp
- ¼ cup chopped green onions (including some tops)
  Salt and pepper
- 1 small French baguette (8 oz.), sliced ¼ inch thick

Heat 1 tablespoon of the oil in an 8- to 10-inch frying pan over medium-high heat. Add whole onions and cook, stirring occasionally, until lightly browned (about 10 minutes). Reduce heat to medium; add corn, vinegar, and sugar. Cook, shaking pan often, until liquid has evaporated and onions are slightly browner (about 5 more minutes). Add roasted peppers and remaining 2 tablespoons oil, stirring until hot. Transfer to a bowl.

Scatter shrimp and green onions over vegetable mixture. Season to taste with salt and pepper. Offer with baguette slices. Makes about 2 dozen appetizers.

Per appetizer: 60 calories, 2 g protein, 8 g carbohydrates, 2 g total fat, 10 mg cholesterol, 70 mg sodium

---

Pictured on facing page

SALSA POTATO SKINS

◆

Preparation time: About 30 minutes
Cooking time: About 1¼ hours

These golden potato skins, coated with Cheddar and jack cheese, are almost a meal in themselves. Offer them with a green chile salsa for bite.

   Chile Salsa (recipe follows)
- 5 **large russet potatoes (about 3 lbs. *total*), scrubbed**
- ⅓ **cup butter or margarine, melted**
- ¾ **cup *each* shredded mild Cheddar and jack cheese**
  Cilantro (coriander) sprigs (optional)

Prepare Chile Salsa; set aside.

Pierce potatoes in several places with a fork. Bake in a 400° oven until soft when pressed (about 1 hour). Let potatoes stand until cool enough to handle. Cut each lengthwise into quarters. With a spoon, scoop out flesh, leaving a ⅛-inch-thick shell; reserve flesh for other uses.

Brush skins inside and out with butter. Place, skin sides down, in a single layer on a 12- by 15-inch baking sheet. Bake in a 500° oven until crisp (about 12 minutes). Remove from oven and evenly sprinkle with both Cheddar and jack.

Broil 4 inches below heat until cheese is melted (about 2 minutes). Arrange on a platter. Garnish with cilantro, if desired. Offer with salsa for dipping. Makes 20 appetizers.

Per appetizer: 115 calories, 3 g protein, 12 g carbohydrates, 6 g total fat, 16 mg cholesterol, 85 mg sodium

Chile Salsa. Stir together 1 can (8 oz.) **tomato sauce**, 1 can (4 oz.) diced **green chiles**, and ¼ cup chopped **green onions** (including tops). If made ahead, cover and refrigerate until next day. Makes 1½ cups.

Per tablespoon: 5 calories, .2 g protein, 1 g carbohydrates, 0 g total fat, 0 mg cholesterol, 103 mg sodium

---

TWICE-BAKED CREAMERS

◆

Preparation time: About 15 minutes
Cooking time: About 1 hour and 5 minutes

Potato purée seasoned with blue cheese and fresh chives fills small red potatoes, often called creamers, in this sophisticated version of twice-baked potatoes.

You can prepare this recipe up to 6 hours ahead of time. Serve the potatoes warm.

- 12 **small red thin-skinned potatoes (*each* 1- to 1½-in. diameter), scrubbed**
- 6 **ounces Gorgonzola cheese**
- 1 **tablespoon chopped chives or green onion (including top)**
- ¼ **teaspoon ground nutmeg**
  Salt and pepper

Pierce potatoes in several places with a fork and place in a 10- by 15-inch baking pan. Bake in a 350° oven until potatoes are soft when pressed (about 1 hour).

Let potatoes stand until cool enough to handle; then cut each potato in half and scoop out flesh, leaving a ¼-inch-thick shell all around. Place flesh in a bowl and add cheese, chives, and nutmeg. Mash until mixture is smooth.

Mound potato mixture in shells and place, filled sides up, in pan. (At this point, you may let stand for up to 2 hours at room temperature; or cover and refrigerate for up to 6 hours.)

Broil 4 to 6 inches below heat until centers are warm and tops are browned (about 4 minutes). Season to taste with salt and pepper. Makes 2 dozen appetizers.

Per appetizer: 44 calories, 2 g protein, 4 g carbohydrates, 2 g total fat, 5 mg cholesterol, 101 mg sodium

Present Salsa Potato Skins (recipe on facing page)
temptingly hot from the broiler. The crisply baked skins
are sprinkled with shredded Cheddar and jack cheese,
and served with an easy-to-make salsa.

CHEESE-STUFFED SQUASH BLOSSOMS

◆

Preparation time: About 30 minutes
Cooking time: About 15 minutes

Enjoy delicate squash blossoms with a zesty chile-cheese stuffing. Look for the blossoms during the summer in specialty produce stores or in Latin American or Mediterranean markets; use them within a day of purchase.

15 to 20 squash blossoms (*each about 3 in. long from base to tip*)
1 small package (3 oz.) cream cheese, at room temperature
1 tablespoon milk
⅓ cup grated Parmesan cheese
Dash of ground black pepper
1½ tablespoons canned diced green chiles
All-purpose flour
2 eggs
1 tablespoon water
Salad oil

Rinse blossoms with cool water; shake off excess. Gently pat dry with paper towels. Trim off stems. Remove stamens, if necessary, to enlarge cavity before stuffing. Set aside.

Beat cream cheese, milk, Parmesan, pepper, and chiles until blended. Spoon about 1 teaspoon of the mixture into each blossom; twist tips to close. Roll in flour to coat lightly; set aside.

In a small bowl, beat eggs and water. Heat ¼ inch oil in a wide frying pan over medium-high heat. When oil is hot, use a fork to dip blossoms, one at a time, into egg mixture. Cook 2 or 3 at a time, turning occasionally, until golden (about 2 minutes). Drain on paper towels. Makes 15 to 20 appetizers.

Per appetizer: 49 calories, 2 g protein, 1 g carbohydrates, 4 g total fat, 30 mg cholesterol, 53 mg sodium

---

Pictured on page 43

RICE-STUFFED SUMMER SQUASH

◆

Preparation time: About 45 minutes
Cooking time: About 45 minutes

Scalloped summer squash make attractive holders for a rich filling of sausage, shallots, cheese, and rice.

24 small scalloped summer squash (2 lbs. *total*)
2 tablespoons olive oil
1 mild Italian sausage (about 3 oz.), casing removed
2 tablespoons finely chopped shallots
⅓ cup whipping cream
1 cup cooked rice
5 tablespoons grated Parmesan cheese

Cut about ½ inch from top of each squash; set tops aside. Carefully scoop out flesh, leaving a ¼-inch-thick shell. Finely chop flesh.

Heat oil in a wide frying pan over medium heat. Crumble sausage into pan, add shallots, and cook, stirring, until meat is no longer pink (about 7 minutes). Stir in chopped squash and cook, stirring, until hot (about 3 more minutes). Add cream, increase heat to high, and continue cooking, stirring often, until most of the liquid has evaporated (about 4 more minutes). Stir in rice. Remove from heat and stir in 3 tablespoons of the cheese.

Fill squash shells with meat mixture. Place, filled sides up, in a greased baking dish just large enough to hold them in a single layer. Sprinkle with remaining cheese. Replace squash tops at a slight angle. Cover dish with foil.

Bake in a 350° oven until squash are barely tender when pierced (about 30 minutes). Let cool briefly. Makes 2 dozen appetizers.

Per appetizer: 54 calories, 2 g protein, 4 g carbohydrates, 4 g total fat, 7 mg cholesterol, 47 mg sodium

---

PISTACHIO-TOPPED ZUCCHINI

◆

Preparation time: About 20 minutes
Cooking time: About 30 minutes

Crunchy pistachios combine with jack cheese, sautéed onions, and mustard seeds to create a tempting topping for sliced zucchini. Add whole pistachios for garnish.

2 medium-size zucchini (about 9 oz. *total*), ends trimmed
3 tablespoons olive oil
1 small onion, finely chopped
2 cloves garlic, minced or pressed
2 teaspoons mustard seeds
¾ cup shelled salted pistachios
1 egg
¾ cup shredded jack cheese

Cut each zucchini diagonally into 10 equal-size slices. Set aside.

Heat 1 tablespoon of the oil in a wide frying pan over medium-high heat. Add onion, garlic, and mustard seeds and cook, stirring often, until onion is lightly browned (about 5 minutes); let cool. Reserving 20 whole pistachios for garnish, chop remaining nuts and stir into onion mixture with egg and cheese.

Generously brush zucchini with remaining 2 tablespoons oil. Arrange, slightly apart, in a 10- by 15-inch baking pan. Bake in a 400° oven, turning after 5 minutes, until golden (about 10 minutes total). Remove from oven; reduce temperature to 325°.

Evenly spoon filling on zucchini. Top each with a whole pistachio. Bake until filling is light golden (about 15 more minutes). Makes 20 appetizers.

Per appetizer: 71 calories, 2 g protein, 2 g carbohydrates, 6 g total fat, 14 mg cholesterol, 64 mg sodium

Pictured on page 46

PARMESAN ZUCCHINI STICKS

◆

Preparation time: About 35 minutes
Cooking time: About 25 minutes

Zucchini sticks are baked, rather than fried, to crisp perfection in a cheese-crumb crust seasoned with sage and rosemary.

- ⅔ cup grated Parmesan cheese
- ½ cup fine dry seasoned bread crumbs
- 1 teaspoon *each* ground sage and dry rosemary
- 2 eggs
- 5 medium-size zucchini (about 1½ lbs. *total*), ends trimmed
- 1 tablespoon olive or salad oil
  Salt
  Sage and rosemary sprigs (optional)

In a bowl, mix cheese, bread crumbs, ground sage, and dry rosemary; set aside. In another bowl, beat eggs until blended.

Cut each zucchini in half crosswise; then cut lengthwise into quarters. Add to eggs and mix gently. Lift out, one at a time, drain briefly, and roll in cheese mixture to coat evenly.

Lay sticks slightly apart in a greased 10- by 15-inch baking pan. Drizzle with oil. Bake in a 450° oven until coating is well browned and crusty (about 25 minutes). Season to taste with salt.

Arrange zucchini sticks in a serving dish and garnish with sage and rosemary sprigs, if desired. Makes 40 appetizers.

Per appetizer: 21 calories, 1 g protein, 2 g carbohydrates, 1 g total fat, 12 mg cholesterol, 68 mg sodium

CARAMELIZED GARLIC & CREAM CHEESE PRUNES

◆

Preparation time: About 30 minutes
Cooking time: About 1¼ hours

Slow-roasting turns whole garlic heads into a surprisingly sweet seasoning that enhances the cream cheese filling for bacon-wrapped prunes.

  Caramelized Garlic Cloves (recipe follows)
- 30 pitted prunes (8 to 12 oz. *total*)
- ½ cup dry red wine
- 1 large package (8 oz.) cream cheese, at room temperature
- 15 slices bacon, cut in half

Prepare Caramelized Garlic Cloves.

In a 1- to 1½-quart pan, bring prunes and wine to a boil over medium heat. Reduce heat, cover, and simmer until prunes are plump (about 7 minutes). Drain; set aside.

Beat cream cheese and garlic cloves until smooth. Make a depression in center of each prune and fill each with about 1 teaspoon of the cheese mixture. Wrap a half-slice of bacon around each prune so ends are on bottom.

Set prunes, filled sides down, on a rack in a 10- by 15-inch broiler or baking pan. Broil about 4 inches below heat just until bacon begins to brown (about 3 minutes). Turn and continue broiling until bacon is crisp (about 3 more minutes). Let stand on rack in pan until cheese is slightly firm (about 2 minutes). Makes 2½ dozen appetizers.

Caramelized Garlic Cloves. Cut 2 large heads **garlic** (*each* about 2½ in. wide) in half crosswise about ⅓ of the way from root end. Pour 1 tablespoon **salad oil** into an 8- or 9-inch square baking pan. Place garlic, cut sides down, in pan. Bake in a 350° oven until center cloves are very soft when pressed and cut sides are browned (about 1 hour). Let cool.

Squeeze whole head to force out soft cloves (remove any bits of husk). If made ahead, cover and refrigerate for up to 3 days; freeze for longer storage. Makes about ¼ cup.

Per appetizer: 73 calories, 2 g protein, 7 g carbohydrates, 5 g total fat, 11 mg cholesterol, 74 mg sodium

BACON-WRAPPED DATES

◆

Preparation time: About 10 minutes
Cooking time: About 10 minutes

How could something so simple be so delicious? Try this recipe and you'll see for yourself.

- 8 slices bacon, cut in half
- 16 pitted dates

Place bacon on a rimmed 10- by 15-inch baking sheet and broil about 6 inches below heat until partially cooked but still soft (about 2½ minutes). Let drain on paper towels. Discard excess fat from baking sheet.

Place a date at end of each bacon slice and roll up. Arrange, seam sides down, on baking sheet. Bake in a 400° oven until bacon is crisp and dates are hot (about 7 minutes). Makes 16 appetizers.

Per appetizer: 41 calories, 1 g protein, 6 g carbohydrates, 2 g total fat, 3 mg cholesterol, 51 mg sodium

*Our selection of cold appetizers comes together for a
festive atmosphere. Sample pistachio-topped Lean
Terrine (recipe on page 79), airy Savory Feta Cheesecake
(recipe on page 73), and colorful Cherry Tomatoes
with Smoked Oysters (recipe on page 84).*

COLD BITES

Not everything that's delicious has to come hot from the oven. Many appetizers, such as glorious meat terrines, tempting marinated fish salads, and delectable vegetable combinations, actually taste best served either at room temperature or straight from the refrigerator.

Cold hors d'oeuvres have their advantages. Frequently, these selections don't require the host or hostess's attention at the last minute or during the party. They can be transported easily to locations far from the kitchen. Moreover, many cold choices wait patiently in the refrigerator for unexpected company or for between-meal snacks. And they're definitely a refreshing and welcome delight when the weather turns warm.

CREAMY DEVILED EGGS

Preparation time: About 15 minutes
Chilling time: At least 1 hour

This basic deviled egg recipe mixes egg yolks with sour cream and mustard. The variations that follow offer some unusual twists on the familiar theme.

- **6 hard-cooked eggs, shelled and cut in half lengthwise**
- **3 tablespoons sour cream**
- **½ teaspoon dry mustard**
  Dash of ground red pepper (cayenne) or liquid hot pepper seasoning
  Salt
  Parsley sprigs or slices of green or ripe olives

Remove yolks from eggs and mash with a fork. Stir in sour cream, mustard, and pepper until well blended. Season to taste with salt. Fill egg whites evenly with yolk mixture and garnish with parsley.

Arrange eggs in a single layer in a deep dish; cover and refrigerate for at least 1 hour or until next day. Makes 1 dozen appetizers.

Per appetizer: 45 calories, 3 g protein, .5 g carbohydrates, 3 g total fat, 108 mg cholesterol, 33 mg sodium

Anchovy Celery Eggs

Follow directions for **Creamy Deviled Eggs,** but omit mustard and salt. Add 1 teaspoon **anchovy paste** and 6 tablespoons finely chopped **celery** to yolk mixture.

Per appetizer: 47 calories, 3 g protein, .6 g carbohydrates, 3 g total fat, 108 mg cholesterol, 55 mg sodium

Dilled Eggs

Follow directions for **Creamy Deviled Eggs,** adding 2 tablespoons chopped **dill pickle** to yolk mixture.

Per appetizer: 45 calories, 3 g protein, .5 g carbohydrates, 3 g total fat, 108 mg cholesterol, 56 mg sodium

Caviar Eggs

Follow directions for **Creamy Deviled Eggs,** but omit mustard and garnish. Add 1 teaspoon **lemon juice** to yolk mixture. Garnish each egg half with ¼ teaspoon drained **red** or black **caviar.**

Per appetizer: 48 calories, 4 g protein, .5 g carbohydrates, 3 g total fat, 116 mg cholesterol, 53 mg sodium

Pictured on page 91

MARBLED TEA EGGS

Preparation time: About 15 minutes
Cooking time: About 1 hour and 40 minutes
Chilling time: At least 8 hours

Here's a great way to begin an Asian-inspired feast. These eggs can be served quartered; or, to let guests admire their delicate marbling, you can leave them whole.

- **8 eggs**
- **3 black-tea bags or 3 teaspoons loose black tea**
- **2 tablespoons soy sauce**
- **1 tablespoon salt**
- **1 whole star anise; or 1 teaspoon anise seeds and 1 cinnamon stick (about 2 in. long)**

Place eggs in a 5-quart pan and cover with cold water. Simmer over medium-high heat for 20 minutes. Drain; rinse eggs under cold running water until cool enough to handle. Gently crack shells with back of a spoon until there's a fine network of cracks, but do not remove shells.

Return eggs to pan. Add 4 cups water, tea, soy, salt, and star anise. Bring to a simmer over medium-high heat. Reduce heat and cook for 1 hour. Let cool; then refrigerate eggs in their cooking liquid for at least 8 hours or up to 2 days. Shell before serving. Makes 8 appetizers.

Per appetizer: 75 calories, 6 g protein, .7 g carbohydrates, 5 g total fat, 213 mg cholesterol, 243 mg sodium

PICKLED QUAIL EGGS & BABY BEETS

Preparation time: About 15 minutes
Cooking time: About 7 minutes
Chilling time: At least 3 hours

Pickled eggs, a pub lunch staple, become appetizer fare when made with quail eggs. Remember to shake the eggs' container occasionally for consistent ruby-red color.

- **Hard-cooked Quail Eggs (directions follow)**
- **1 can (8¼ oz.) pickled baby beets**
- **8 black peppercorns**
- **2 tablespoons minced red onion**
- **1 tablespoon chopped fresh dill or 1 teaspoon dill weed**

Prepare Hard-cooked Quail Eggs.

Drain beet juice into a 1½- to 2-quart pan. Add peppercorns and bring to a boil over high heat. Meanwhile, place beets and eggs in a 4-cup jar. Let juice cool slightly. Then pour into jar, cover, and refrigerate for at least 3 hours or up to 2 days, shaking jar gently several times or inverting occasionally.

Drain off liquid and pour beets and eggs into a small bowl; sprinkle with onion and dill. Offer with wooden picks. Makes 10 to 12 appetizers.

Hard-cooked Quail Eggs. Place 10 to 12 **quail eggs** in a single layer in a 1- to 1½-quart pan. Cover with **water.** Bring to a boil over high heat; immediately reduce heat to hold water just below simmering and cook eggs for 5 minutes. Drain. Immerse eggs in cold water; then crack shells with back of a spoon and remove shells.

Per appetizer: 29 calories, 1 g protein, 4 g carbohydrates, 1 g total fat, 76 mg cholesterol, 56 mg sodium

Pictured on page 70

SAVORY FETA CHEESECAKE

Preparation time: About 20 minutes
Cooking time: About 45 minutes

No delicate dessert cake, this cheesecake boasts a distinctive feta cheese filling in a whole wheat pastry.

Whole Wheat Press-in Pastry (recipe follows)
1 pound feta cheese
1 large package (8 oz.) cream cheese, at room temperature
3 eggs
Whole Greek olives or thinly sliced green onions (including tops)
Oregano sprigs (optional)

Prepare Whole Wheat Press-in Pastry; set aside.

Cut feta and cream cheese into about 1-inch chunks. In a food processor or blender, whirl feta, cream cheese, and eggs until smooth. Pour into pastry. Bake in a 350° oven until center barely jiggles when gently shaken (about 20 minutes). Let cool to room temperature in pan on a wire rack. If made ahead, cover and refrigerate for up to 2 days; bring to room temperature before serving.

Remove pan sides. Garnish with olives and, if desired, oregano; cut into wedges. Makes 16 appetizers.

Whole Wheat Press-in Pastry.
Combine 1 cup **whole wheat flour** and 6 tablespoons firm **butter** or margarine, cut up. With your fingers, rub mixture together until butter lumps are no longer distinguishable. With a fork, stir in 1 **egg** and mix until dough forms a ball.

Press dough in a firm, even layer over bottom and about 1¾ inches up sides of a 9-inch round spring-form pan or cake pan with removable bottom. Bake in a 350° oven for about 20 minutes or until lightly browned. Use hot or cold.

Per appetizer: 206 calories, 8 g protein, 7 g carbohydrates, 17 g total fat, 106 mg cholesterol, 418 mg sodium

ZUCCHINI FRITTATA

Preparation time: About 20 minutes
Cooking time: About 1¼ hours
Chilling time: At least 2 hours

Flavored with fresh basil, parsley, sautéed onions, and Parmesan cheese, this baked zucchini omelet is chilled and served cold.

2 tablespoons olive oil
2 tablespoons butter or margarine
2 medium-size onions, finely chopped
2 cloves garlic, minced or pressed
½ cup chopped parsley
8 medium-size zucchini (about 2¼ lbs. *total*), shredded
2 tablespoons chopped fresh basil leaves or 1½ teaspoons dry basil leaves
½ cup grated Parmesan cheese
Salt and pepper
16 eggs

Heat oil and butter in a wide frying pan over medium heat. Add onions, garlic, and parsley; cook, stirring often, until onions are soft (about 7 minutes). Add zucchini; cook, stirring, until liquid has evaporated (about 20 more minutes). Remove from heat and stir in basil and Parmesan; season to taste with salt and pepper.

In a large bowl, beat eggs until blended. Stir in zucchini mixture. Spread in a greased shallow 3-quart casserole. Bake in a 350° oven until firm in center when lightly touched (about 45 minutes). Let cool on a wire rack. Cover and refrigerate for at least 2 hours or until next day.

Cut into serving pieces. Makes 1 dozen appetizers.

Per appetizer: 170 calories, 11 g protein, 5 g carbohydrates, 12 g total fat, 291 mg cholesterol, 169 mg sodium

Pictured on page 3

COCKTAIL CREAM PUFFS

Preparation time: About 50 minutes
Cooking time: About 25 minutes
Chilling time: At least 2 hours

Tiny cream puffs elegantly cradle ginger-flavored chicken salad.

Gingered Chicken Salad (recipe follows)
1 cup water
½ cup (¼ lb.) butter or margarine
1 cup all-purpose flour
4 eggs

Prepare Gingered Chicken Salad.

In a 2- to 3-quart pan, stir water and butter over medium-high heat until butter is melted. Add flour all at once, stirring until mixture leaves sides of pan and forms a ball (about 2 minutes). Remove from heat and transfer to a bowl; let cool briefly.

Add eggs, one at a time, beating well after each addition. Drop 1 tablespoon of the dough for each puff onto greased baking sheets, spacing puffs about 2 inches apart. Bake in a 400° oven until golden (about 20 minutes). Turn off oven. Pierce each puff in several places. Return to oven until crisp (about 10 minutes). Let cool on wire racks.

Split puffs horizontally. Evenly fill with chicken salad. Replace tops. If made ahead, cover and refrigerate for up to 2 hours. Makes about 3 dozen appetizers.

Gingered Chicken Salad. Mix ½ cup **mayonnaise**, ½ teaspoon **dry mustard**, and 1 teaspoon grated **fresh ginger** or ¼ teaspoon ground ginger. Stir in 2 cups chopped **cooked chicken**, ½ cup chopped and drained canned **water chestnuts**, and 2 **green onions** (including tops), thinly sliced. Cover and refrigerate for at least 2 hours or until next day.

Per appetizer: 82 calories, 3 g protein, 3 g carbohydrates, 6 g total fat, 39 mg cholesterol, 57 mg sodium

Pictured on facing page

TOMATO TARTS NIÇOISE

**Preparation time: About 55 minutes
Cooking time: About 50 minutes
Chilling time: At least 3 hours**

Bring sunny Mediterranean flavors to your table with these savory tarts.

    Cheese Pastry (recipe follows)
4 **tablespoons olive oil**
2 **large onions, slivered**
1 **large can (28 oz.) tomatoes**
½ **teaspoon** *each* **sugar and dry rosemary**
⅛ **teaspoon** *each* **ground red pepper (cayenne) and black pepper**
2 **cloves garlic, minced or pressed**
2 **cans (2 oz.** *each***) flat anchovy fillets**
32 **Niçoise or medium-size ripe olives**
    Rosemary sprigs (optional)

Prepare Cheese Pastry and divide into 8 equal portions; roll each out into a circle to fit 4-inch tart pans ¾ to 1 inch deep. Line pans with pastry, trimming edges even with top.

    Heat 2 tablespoons of the oil in a wide frying pan over medium heat; add onions and cook, stirring occasionally, until golden and very soft (about 15 minutes). Evenly spoon onions into pastry-lined pans.

    In pan, heat remaining 2 tablespoons oil slightly; add tomatoes (break up with a spoon) and their liquid, sugar, rosemary, red pepper, black pepper, and garlic. Cook over high heat, stirring occasionally, until mixture is reduced to about 2 cups (about 15 minutes). Evenly spoon into pastry. Arrange 2 anchovy fillets and 4 olives on each tart.

    Bake in a 450° oven until well browned (about 20 minutes). Let stand for 10 minutes. Tip tarts out of pans and place on a rack to cool completely. Cover and refrigerate for at least 3 hours or until next day.

    Arrange on a platter and garnish with rosemary sprigs, if desired. Makes 8 appetizers.

Cheese Pastry. Stir together 1½ cups **all-purpose flour,** ½ teaspoon **salt,** and ¼ cup **grated Parmesan cheese.** Cut in 4 tablespoons firm **butter** or margarine and 4 tablespoons **solid vegetable shortening** until mixture resembles coarse crumbs. With a fork, gradually stir in 2 to 3 tablespoons **cold water** until mixture holds together. Smooth into a flat ball.

Per appetizer: 351 calories, 8 g protein, 26 g carbohydrates, 24 g total fat, 30 mg cholesterol, 926 mg sodium

CARPACCIO

**Preparation time: About 45 minutes
Freezing time: About 1½ hours**

Carpaccio—thinly sliced raw beef—is wrapped around breadsticks.

1¼ **pounds first-cut top round, trimmed of fat, if necessary**
½ **cup mayonnaise**
⅓ **cup Dijon mustard**
1 **teaspoon Worcestershire**
2 **teaspoons lime or lemon juice**
    Dash of ground red pepper (cayenne)
60 **breadsticks**
    Lime or lemon wedges

Wrap meat and freeze just until firm (about 1½ hours). Meanwhile, mix mayonnaise, mustard, Worcestershire, lime juice, and pepper until smooth; cover and refrigerate.

    Up to 2 hours before serving, use a food slicer to cut frozen beef across grain into paper-thin slices. (Or, using a very sharp knife, slice beef as thinly as possible; then place slices, a few at a time, between pieces of plastic wrap and pound with flat side of a mallet until paper thin.) As meat is prepared, arrange slices, separated by plastic wrap, in a large pan.

    Cut each slice of beef in half lengthwise; wrap around a breadstick. Offer with sauce and lime. Makes about 5 dozen appetizers.

Per appetizer: 47 calories, 3 g protein, 4 g carbohydrates, 2 g total fat, 7 mg cholesterol, 91 mg sodium

Pictured on page 83

CHEDDAR CHEESE PUFFS

**Preparation time: About 1 hour
Cooking time: About 35 minutes**

Smoked trout folded into horseradish-accented whipped cream creates the rich filling for delicate puffs.

1 **cup water**
½ **cup (¼ lb.) butter or margarine**
⅛ **teaspoon ground nutmeg**
1 **cup all-purpose flour**
4 **eggs**
½ **cup lightly packed finely shredded sharp Cheddar cheese**
    Smoked Trout Mousse (recipe follows)

In a 2- to 3-quart pan, stir water, butter, and nutmeg over medium-high heat until butter is melted. Add flour all at once, stirring until mixture leaves sides of pan and forms a ball (about 2 minutes). Remove from heat and transfer to a bowl; let cool briefly.

    Add eggs, one at a time, beating well after each addition. Stir in cheese. Drop by spoonfuls about 1½ inches in diameter onto greased baking sheets, spacing puffs about 2 inches apart. Bake in a 400° oven until golden (about 20 minutes). Turn off oven. Pierce each puff in several places. Return to oven until crisp (about 10 minutes). Let cool.

    Meanwhile, prepare Smoked Trout Mousse. Split puffs horizontally. Evenly fill with mousse; then replace tops. If made ahead, cover and refrigerate for up to 2 hours. Makes about 3 dozen appetizers.

Smoked Trout Mousse. Beat 1 cup **whipping cream,** 1½ tablespoons **lemon juice,** and ⅛ teaspoon *each* **salt** and **ground white pepper** until stiff. Fold in 1 tablespoon **prepared horseradish** and ⅔ cup finely chopped boneless, skinless **smoked trout.**

Per appetizer: 73 calories, 2 g protein, 3 g carbohydrates, 6 g total fat, 42 mg cholesterol, 77 mg sodium

Summer calls for easy entertaining. Relax with refreshing Citrus Spritzer (recipe on page 88), chilled Tomato Tarts Niçoise (recipe on facing page), make-ahead Turkey-Cheese Pinwheels (recipe on page 77), and simple-to-prepare Snap Pea Knots (recipe on page 92).

FISHLESS SASHIMI

Preparation time: About 15 minutes
Marinating time: About 45 minutes

Lean beef tenderloin, flavored with a peppery oyster sauce marinade, replaces raw fish in this version of sashimi.

- 1 **pound lean beef tenderloin, trimmed of fat**
- 3 **tablespoons** *each* **oyster sauce and lemon juice**
- ¼ **teaspoon** *each* **ground red pepper (cayenne) and finely chopped onion**
  Chopped parsley

Cut beef into very thin slices; then cut slices into bite-size pieces. Place meat in a bowl and stir in oyster sauce, lemon juice, pepper, and onion. Cover and refrigerate until meat has lost all its bright red color (about 45 minutes).

Arrange meat pieces on a serving platter; sprinkle with parsley. Makes about 8 servings.

Per serving: 94 calories, 12 g protein, 2 g carbohydrates, 4 g total fat, 35 mg cholesterol, 300 mg sodium

PASTRAMI ROLL-UPS

Preparation time: About 10 minutes

This tasty appetizer is a snap to prepare. Simply roll thin slices of pastrami around horseradish-flavored cream cheese. You can substitute Lebanon bologna for the pastrami, if you like.

- 1 **small package (3 oz.) cream cheese, at room temperature**
- ¾ **teaspoon prepared horseradish**
- ¼ **pound pastrami slices**

Beat cream cheese and horseradish until smooth. Spread cheese mixture evenly on pastrami slices; roll up jelly roll style. Cut into bite-size pieces. Makes about 16 appetizers.

Per appetizer: 26 calories, 2 g protein, .6 g carbohydrates, 2 g total fat, 9 mg cholesterol, 106 mg sodium

VEAL & OLIVE TERRINE

Preparation time: About 20 minutes
Cooking time: About 1½ hours
Chilling time: At least 8 hours

Slices of this delicate veal meatloaf display a layer of pimento-stuffed green olives. Plan to make this terrine ahead of time; the flavors need time to blend. Accompany with thin slices of French bread.

- 2 **tablespoons butter or margarine**
- 2 **large onions, finely chopped**
- 2 **cloves garlic, minced or pressed**
- 30 **pimento-stuffed green olives**
- 2 **eggs**
- ¼ **cup fine dry bread crumbs**
- 1 **teaspoon dry basil leaves**
- ½ **teaspoon salt**
- ⅛ **teaspoon ground white pepper**
- ¾ **pound ground veal**
- ½ **pound ground pork**
- 3 **bay leaves**

In a wide frying pan, melt butter over medium heat. Add onions and cook, stirring often, until soft (about 7 minutes). Stir in garlic; remove pan from heat and let cool briefly. Finely chop half the olives, reserving remaining olives whole.

In a large bowl, beat eggs. Mix in bread crumbs, basil, salt, and pepper. Add onion mixture, chopped olives, veal, and pork; mix until blended. Spread half the mixture in a deep, straight-sided 4½- to 5-cup terrine or baking pan. Arrange whole olives in 2 or 3 rows down length of pan. Spread remaining meat mixture over olives. Top with bay leaves.

Cover pan and place in a larger pan. Put in a 350° oven and pour scalding water into larger pan to a depth of at least 1 inch. Bake until meat is firm when pressed and juices run clear when a knife is inserted in center (about 1 hour and 20 minutes). Let cool; then cover and refrigerate for at least 8 hours or up to 5 days.

Just before serving, remove and discard solid fat and bay leaves. Cut terrine into ¼-inch-thick slices and lift carefully from pan. Makes about 1 dozen appetizers.

Per appetizer: 136 calories, 11 g protein, 4 g carbohydrates, 8 g total fat, 78 mg cholesterol, 375 mg sodium

PROSCIUTTO & PEA BUNDLES

Preparation time: About 20 minutes
Cooking time: About 30 seconds

Quick cooking is the secret to these snap peas' crunch and color. Use flavored cream cheese for ease in preparing these attractive carrot-topped packages wrapped with prosciutto.

- 60 **sugar snap peas, ends and strings removed**
- 2 **medium-size carrots, peeled**
- 2 **to 3 ounces thinly sliced prosciutto or cooked ham**
- 1 **package (4 oz.) onion-flavored spreadable cream cheese**

In a wide frying pan, cook peas in 2 inches boiling water until bright green (about 30 seconds). Drain, immerse in ice water, and drain again. Set aside.

Cut carrots crosswise into thirds; cut each third into 10 matchstick-size pieces. Cut prosciutto into 60 strips.

Slice each pea along outside seam. Open slightly and push about ½ teaspoon of the cheese into each pea, smoothing cheese with back of a knife. Position a carrot stick on filling, hold in place, and wrap a prosciutto strip in a band around carrot and pea. Makes 5 dozen appetizers.

Per appetizer: 11 calories, .5 g protein, .8 g carbohydrates, .7 g total fat, 2 mg cholesterol, 36 mg sodium

SPINACH-WRAPPED CHICKEN

◆

Preparation time: About 55 minutes
Cooking time: About 15 minutes
Chilling time: At least 1 hour

Wrap fresh spinach leaves around tender chunks of chicken and offer with mayonnaise accented with curry, chutney, and freshly grated orange peel.

- 2 **whole chicken breasts (about 2 lbs.** *total***)**
- 1 **can (14½ oz.) regular-strength chicken broth**
- ¼ **cup soy sauce**
- 1 **tablespoon Worcestershire**
- 1 **bunch spinach (about 1 lb.), stems removed, washed and dried**
- 8 **cups boiling water**
  Curry Mayonnaise (recipe follows)

In a 10-inch frying pan, combine chicken breasts, broth, soy, and Worcestershire. Bring to a boil over medium heat; reduce heat, cover, and simmer until meat in thickest part is no longer pink when cut (about 15 minutes).

Lift chicken from broth and let cool slightly. Remove and discard skin and bones; cut meat into 1-inch chunks.

Place spinach in a colander and pour boiling water over leaves; drain thoroughly. Let cool.

Place a chunk of chicken at stem end of a spinach leaf. Roll over once, fold leaf in on both sides, and continue rolling around chicken. Secure end of leaf with a wooden pick. Refrigerate for at least 1 hour or until next day.

Meanwhile, prepare Curry Mayonnaise. Offer with chicken for dipping. Makes about 4 dozen appetizers.

Per appetizer: 17 calories, 3 g protein, .3 g carbohydrates, .3 g total fat, 8 mg cholesterol, 39 mg sodium

Curry Mayonnaise. Mix ¼ cup *each* **mayonnaise** and **sour cream,** 2 teaspoons **curry powder,** 2 tablespoons chopped **Major Grey's chutney,** and 1 teaspoon **grated orange peel** until smoothly blended. Cover and refrigerate for at least 1 hour. Makes about ⅔ cup.

Per tablespoon: 62 calories, .3 g protein, 3 g carbohydrates, 6 g total fat, 6 mg cholesterol, 41 mg sodium

CHILI-BAKED CHICKEN WINGS

◆

Preparation time: About 35 minutes
Cooking time: About 35 minutes
Chilling time: At least 4 hours

These mini-drumsticks—really the meaty joints of chicken wings—are covered with a crunchy, chili-spiked coating. Because they're served cold, they're perfect for an outdoor party.

- 2 **tablespoons butter or margarine**
- 1 **tablespoon salad oil**
- ¼ **cup all-purpose flour**
- 2 **tablespoons yellow cornmeal**
- 1½ **teaspoons chili powder**
- ½ **teaspoon ground cumin**
- 1¼ **pounds (about 14) chicken drummettes (meatiest part of wing)**

Combine butter and oil in a 10- by 15-inch baking pan. Set in a 400° oven to melt butter. Meanwhile, in a small bag, combine flour, cornmeal, chili powder, and cumin. Add chicken, about half at a time, to bag and shake to coat lightly with seasoned flour. Arrange in pan in a single layer, turning to coat with butter mixture.

Return pan to oven and bake until meat near bone is no longer pink when cut (about 30 minutes). Let cool; cover and refrigerate for at least 4 hours or until next day. Makes about 14 appetizers.

Per appetizer: 89 calories, 7 g protein, 3 g carbohydrates, 6 g total fat, 31 mg cholesterol, 46 mg sodium

Pictured on page 75

TURKEY-CHEESE PINWHEELS

◆

Preparation time: About 20 minutes
Chilling time: At least 3 hours

Lean turkey breast slices swirl around vegetable-accented Neufchâtel cheese in this easy-to-make appetizer. You can make the flavorful pinwheels the day before you plan to serve them.

- 1 **package (8 oz.) Neufchâtel cheese, at room temperature**
- 1 **tablespoon** *each* **chopped chives and prepared horseradish**
- 2 **tablespoons chopped Italian parsley**
- ¼ **teaspoon ground white pepper**
- 1 **medium-size carrot, finely shredded**
- 2 **tablespoons drained diced canned pimentos**
  Salt
- 1 **package (8 oz.) sliced cooked turkey or ham**
  Italian parsley sprigs (optional)

Mix cheese, chives, horseradish, parsley, and pepper until smooth. Blend in carrot and pimentos. Season to taste with salt.

On each turkey slice, spread about 1 rounded tablespoon of the cheese mixture. Starting with a narrow end, roll each slice compactly to make a pinwheel. Place, seam sides down, in a single layer in a shallow pan. Cover and refrigerate for at least 3 hours or until next day.

Cut into 1-inch slices. Arrange on a platter and garnish with parsley sprigs, if desired. Makes about 3 dozen appetizers.

Per appetizer: 25 calories, 2 g protein, .5 g carbohydrates, 2 g total fat, 7 mg cholesterol, 75 mg sodium

*A tangy lime-juice marinade "cooks" raw shellfish
for delicate Scallop Seviche (recipe on facing page).
Guests can spoon the salad into endive leaves and eat
out-of-hand.*

Pictured on page 70

LEAN TERRINE

Preparation time: About 30 minutes
Cooking time: About 1¾ hours
Chilling time: At least 4 hours

Ground turkey and ham are combined with pistachios, onions, and fresh sage in this elegant but light version of meatloaf. Serve thin slices on crusty French bread.

- 2 tablespoons salad oil
- 2 large onions, finely chopped
- 3 cloves garlic, minced or pressed
- 2 tablespoons chopped fresh sage or 1 teaspoon dry sage leaves
- ¼ cup brandy
- 2 large eggs
- ½ cup soft bread crumbs
- ¼ teaspoon *each* ground nutmeg and ground white pepper
- ⅛ teaspoon ground allspice
- ½ cup *each* finely chopped cooked ham and salted pistachios
- 2 pounds ground turkey
  Sage sprigs (optional)

Heat oil in a wide frying pan over medium heat. Add onions and cook, stirring often, until soft (about 7 minutes). Stir in garlic and chopped sage. Remove pan from heat and add brandy; set aflame (not beneath an exhaust fan or near flammable items), shaking pan until flames die. Return to heat and stir until most of the liquid has evaporated; set aside.

In a large bowl, beat eggs. Mix in bread crumbs, nutmeg, pepper, allspice, ham, and pistachios (reserve some for garnish, if desired). Add onion mixture and turkey; mix until blended.

Spread in a 6- to 8-cup terrine or baking pan. Cover and place in a larger pan. Put in a 350° oven and pour scalding water into larger pan to a depth of at least 1 inch. Bake until meat is firm when pressed and juices run clear when a knife is inserted in center (about 1½ hours). Let cool; then cover and refrigerate for at least 4 hours or up to 2 days.

Garnish with sage sprigs and reserved nuts, if desired. Cut terrine into thin slices. Makes about 20 appetizers.

Per appetizer: 127 calories, 11 g protein, 3 g carbohydrates, 8 g total fat, 54 mg cholesterol, 109 mg sodium

CALICO FISH SALAD

Preparation time: About 20 minutes
Cooking time: About 10 minutes

Orange roughy is lightly tossed with mustard, tarragon, and a colorful array of vegetables.

- 1 pound orange roughy or sole fillets
- 3 tablespoons coarse-grained mustard
- ¼ cup celery leaves (optional)
- ⅔ cup *each* diced yellow bell pepper, tomato, and celery
- 2 tablespoons lemon juice
- 2 teaspoons minced fresh tarragon leaves or ½ teaspoon dry tarragon leaves
  Salt and pepper
- 16 inner romaine lettuce leaves, washed and crisped

Rinse fish and pat dry. Arrange in a single layer in an 8- to 9-inch square pan. Spread fillets with mustard and, if desired, top with celery leaves. Cover pan with foil.

Bake in a 400° oven just until fish looks just slightly translucent or wet inside when cut in thickest part (about 10 minutes). Let cool; discard celery leaves, if used. Add bell pepper, tomato, diced celery, lemon juice, and tarragon to fish, mixing gently with a fork and breaking fish into bite-size pieces. Season to taste with salt and pepper. If made ahead, cover and refrigerate until next day.

Place fish salad in a small bowl and surround with lettuce leaves for scooping. Makes 16 appetizers.

Per appetizer: 44 calories, 5 g protein, 1 g carbohydrates, 2 g total fat, 6 mg cholesterol, 52 mg sodium

Pictured on facing page

SCALLOP SEVICHE

Preparation time: About 25 minutes
Chilling time: At least 8 hours

To make seviche, raw fish—in this case, scallops—is marinated with lime juice until it looks and tastes as if poached. Present this refreshingly tangy fish salad with endive leaves for scooping.

- ½ pound sea or bay scallops
- ⅓ cup lime or lemon juice
- ¼ cup diced white onion
- 1 or 2 fresh jalapeño or serrano chiles, stemmed, seeded, and finely diced
- 2 tablespoons salad oil
- ½ teaspoon chopped fresh oregano leaves or ⅛ teaspoon dry oregano leaves
- ½ cup chopped yellow, green, or red bell pepper
- 2 teaspoons minced cilantro (coriander)
  Salt
  Oregano sprigs
  Lime halves or wedges
- 1 large head Belgian endive, separated into leaves, washed and crisped (optional)

Rinse scallops and pat dry. If using sea scallops, cut into ½-inch pieces.

In a large nonmetal bowl, stir together scallops, lime juice, onion, chiles, oil, and chopped oregano. Cover and refrigerate, stirring occasionally, for at least 8 hours or until next day.

Stir bell pepper and cilantro into scallop mixture; season to taste with salt. Pour into a serving bowl and garnish with oregano sprigs. Offer with lime halves and, if desired, endive leaves for scooping. Makes about 6 servings.

Per serving: 82 calories, 7 g protein, 3 g carbohydrates, 5 g total fat, 12 mg cholesterol, 64 mg sodium

Treats that can be prepared with a minimum of fuss and in little time are two times more pleasing. They get the cook out of the kitchen without a lot of effort and satisfy the hungry without a lot of waiting.

Whether after school, after work, before a party, or before a meal, these snacks can be made quickly.

RICE-CRUSTED MINI-PIZZAS

Preparation time: About 10 minutes
Cooking time: About 18 minutes

Crisp rice cakes take the place of traditional yeast dough for individual-size pizzas. Top each with red onion, salami, tomato, and three kinds of cheese to make a hearty snack that will please diners of all ages.

- 2 tablespoons olive oil
- 1 large red onion, thinly sliced
- 1 clove garlic, minced or pressed
- 1 teaspoon dry oregano leaves
- 12 rice cakes (3½-in. diameter)
- 1 package (3 oz.) sliced dry salami, cut into thin strips
- 2 medium-size tomatoes
- ½ cup grated Parmesan cheese
- 1 cup (4 oz.) *each* lightly packed shredded jack and provolone cheese

Heat oil in a wide frying pan over medium-high heat. Add onion and cook, stirring often, until soft and lightly browned (about 8 minutes). Stir in garlic and oregano; remove from heat.

Arrange rice cakes in a single layer on a 12- by 15-inch baking sheet. Top evenly with onion mixture and salami. Cut each tomato cross-

QUICK SNACKS

wise into 6 slices. Place a tomato slice on each pizza and sprinkle with Parmesan, jack, and provolone.

Bake pizzas in a 450° oven until cheese is melted (about 10 minutes). Makes 1 dozen snacks.

Per snack: 177 calories, 9 g protein, 11 g carbohydrates, 11 g total fat, 23 mg cholesterol, 339 mg sodium

PIZZA SNACKS MEXICANA

Preparation time: About 5 minutes
Cooking time: About 8 minutes

Made with tortillas, jack and Cheddar cheese, and green chiles, this snack is more like a Southwestern-style tostada than an Italian-style pizza.

- 3 large (10-in. diameter) flour tortillas
- 1½ cups *each* lightly packed shredded jack and Cheddar cheese
- 1 can (4 oz.) diced green chiles
  Prepared salsa

Place tortillas on 12- by 15-inch baking sheets. Sprinkle each with ½ cup of the jack and ½ cup of the Cheddar. Top evenly with chiles.

Bake tortillas, one at a time, in a 425° oven until crisp and golden brown (about 8 minutes). Cut each into 6 wedges and drizzle with salsa to taste. Makes about 1½ dozen snacks.

Per snack: 94 calories, 5 g protein, 5 g carbohydrates, 6 g total fat, 18 mg cholesterol, 183 mg sodium

MINTED YOGURT DIP

Preparation time: About 5 minutes

Fresh mint perks up a cumin-flavored yogurt dip. Serve it with red and yellow cherry tomatoes.

- 2 tablespoons lightly packed chopped fresh mint leaves or 1 tablespoon dry mint leaves
- ½ cup plain yogurt
- ¼ teaspoon ground cumin
- 24 cherry tomatoes

Mix mint, yogurt, and cumin until blended. If made ahead, cover and refrigerate until next day. Offer with cherry tomatoes for dipping. Makes 2 dozen snacks.

Per snack: 5 calories, .3 g protein, .8 g carbohydrates, .1 g total fat, .3 mg cholesterol, 4 mg sodium

TANGY EGG SALAD

Preparation time: About 5 minutes

When you substitute yogurt for mayonnaise in this egg salad, the results are light and refreshing.

- 4 hard-cooked eggs, shelled and chopped
- 3 tablespoons plain yogurt
- 1 tablespoon sweet pickle relish
- 2 teaspoons prepared mustard
  Salt and pepper
- 12 red leaf lettuce leaves, washed and crisped

Mix eggs, yogurt, relish, and mustard until blended. Season to taste with salt and pepper. Spoon into lettuce leaves. Makes 1 dozen snacks.

Per snack: 31 calories, 2 g protein, 1 g carbohydrates, 2 g total fat, 71 mg cholesterol, 44 mg sodium

CHILLED CUCUMBER CREAM SOUP

Preparation time: About 15 minutes

A blender or food processor makes this soup a snap to prepare. There's no cooking required, so the refreshingly cold result is perfect for a hot day. Serve it in mugs.

Make sure that the cucumbers, yogurt, and sour cream are well chilled before you begin.

- 3 medium-size cucumbers (about 1½ lbs. *total*), peeled and cut into cubes
- 1 clove garlic, cut in half
- 3 tablespoons *each* chopped parsley and chopped onion
- 1 cup regular-strength chicken broth
- 3 tablespoons white wine vinegar
- 2 cups plain yogurt
- 1 cup sour cream
  Salt and pepper

In a blender or food processor, whirl cucumbers, garlic, parsley, onion, broth, and vinegar until well blended. Pour about half the mixture into a container; set aside.

Add 1 cup of the yogurt and ½ cup of the sour cream to cucumber mixture in blender; whirl until smooth. Transfer to a large bowl. Pour reserved cucumber mixture into blender container and add remaining 1 cup yogurt and ½ cup sour cream. Whirl until smooth.

Add to bowl and season to taste with salt and pepper. Makes about 8 servings (¾ cup each).

Per serving: 114 calories, 5 g protein, 8 g carbohydrates, 7 g total fat, 16 mg cholesterol, 183 mg sodium

APRICOT & ALMOND-BUTTER BITES

Preparation time: About 5 minutes

Almond butter, a sophisticated relative of peanut butter, is sandwiched between dried apricot halves in these deliciously simple snacks.

- 1 package (6 oz.) dried apricots
- ¼ to ⅓ cup almond butter

Set aside half the apricot halves. On cut side of each of the remaining apricot halves, evenly spread about ½ teaspoon of the almond butter. Top each with one of the remaining apricot halves, smooth side up. Makes about 2 dozen snacks.

Per snack: 36 calories, .7 g protein, 5 g carbohydrates, 2 g total fat, 0 mg cholesterol, 14 mg sodium

STRAWBERRY-BANANA SLURP

Preparation time: About 10 minutes

This fruit and yogurt smoothie is a refreshing way to grab a snack. Simply add a straw and drink up!

- 1 cup plain yogurt
- ½ cup *each* orange juice and crushed ice
- 2 cups sliced, hulled strawberries
- 1 medium-size ripe banana, peeled and sliced
- 2 tablespoons sugar

In a blender, whirl yogurt, orange juice, ice, strawberries, banana, and sugar until well blended. Makes 4 servings (about 1 cup each).

Per serving: 123 calories, 4 g protein, 26 g carbohydrates, 1 g total fat, 3 mg cholesterol, 41 mg sodium

NEEDLES IN A HAYSTACK

Preparation time: About 5 minutes

For a party treat or after-school nibble, simply pull string cheese into fine strips and mix them with crisp pretzel sticks.

- 1½ ounces string cheese
- 2 ounces (about 1½ cups) pretzel sticks

Pull cheese into fine strips ¹⁄₁₆ to ⅛ inch wide. Mix in a bowl with pretzels. Makes about 4 servings.

Per serving: 89 calories, 4 g protein, 13 g carbohydrates, 1 g total fat, 6 mg cholesterol, 313 mg sodium

HONEYED PEANUT BUTTER WRAP-UPS

Preparation time: About 5 minutes

This snack can bring out the child in almost anyone. It's the perfect pick-me-up for after school or after work.

- ¼ cup creamy or crunchy peanut butter
- 4 lettuce leaves, washed and crisped
- ¼ cup raisins
- 2 tablespoons honey

For each serving, spread 1 tablespoon of the peanut butter on a lettuce leaf. Sprinkle with 1 tablespoon of the raisins and top with ½ tablespoon of the honey. Wrap or roll lettuce leaf around filling. Makes 4 snacks.

Per snack: 156 calories, 5 g protein, 19 g carbohydrates, 8 g total fat, 0 mg cholesterol, 78 mg sodium

PICKLED HERRING

Preparation time: **About 10 minutes**
Marinating time: **At least 1 day**

Easy to prepare, this traditional Swedish dish must be made ahead. Serve it on slices of hearty dark bread with plenty of sour cream.

- 1½ **cups or 2 jars (6 to 8 oz.** *each***) marinated or wine-flavored herring fillet pieces**
- 1 **carrot, thinly sliced**
- 1 **small red onion, thinly sliced**
- 1 **teaspoon whole allspice, slightly crushed**
- ⅓ **cup distilled white vinegar**
- 1 **cup water**
- ⅔ **cup sugar**
- 1 **bay leaf**

Drain liquid from herring. Alternate layers of herring, carrot, onion, and allspice in a deep 4-cup container until all are used. In a small bowl, stir together vinegar, water, and sugar; pour over herring. Tuck in bay leaf. Cover and refrigerate for at least a day or up to 4 days. Makes about 2½ dozen appetizers.

Per appetizer: 44 calories, 1 g protein, 6 g carbohydrates, 2 g total fat, 1 mg cholesterol, 83 mg sodium

CUCUMBER WITH GOLDEN CAVIAR

Preparation time: **About 15 minutes**

The holder is as elegant as the filling when you cut cucumbers into tulip-shaped cups to carry sour cream topped with golden caviar.

- 2 **Japanese cucumbers or 1 long, slender English cucumber (about 1 lb.** *total***)**
- ¼ **to ⅓ cup sour cream**
- ¼ **to ⅓ cup golden whitefish caviar or other caviar**
  Lime juice

Cut stem end of cucumber flat. Hold vertically; about 1½ inches up from flat end, insert a knife tip at a 45° angle and make 3 equally spaced cuts to center. Pull to release cup.

Trim pointed end flat and repeat cuts to make a total of 16 cups. (At this point, you may cover and refrigerate for up to 2 days.)

Spoon ½ to 1 teaspoon of the sour cream into each cucumber cup and top with ½ to 1 teaspoon of the caviar. Sprinkle with lime juice. Makes 16 appetizers.

Per appetizer: 24 calories, 1 g protein, 1 g carbohydrates, 2 g total fat, 29 mg cholesterol, 72 mg sodium

Pictured on facing page

SMOKED SALMON MAYONNAISE

Preparation time: **About 15 minutes**
Chilling time: **At least 1 hour**

Smoked salmon flavors fresh mayonnaise made in your blender or food processor. Spoon the elegant mixture on cucumber slices.

- ½ **cup (about 4 oz.) chopped smoked salmon or lox**
- 1 **egg yolk**
- 1½ **tablespoons lemon juice**
- 3 **tablespoons salad oil**
- 1 **long, slender English cucumber (about 1 lb.), cut into ⅛-inch-thick slices**
  Finely chopped mild red onion

In a blender or food processor, whirl salmon, egg yolk, and lemon juice until puréed. With motor running, add oil in a thin, steady stream, mixing until smoothly blended. Cover and refrigerate for at least 1 hour or until next day.

Pipe or spoon about 1 teaspoon of the salmon mixture onto each cucumber slice. If made ahead, cover and refrigerate for up to 2 hours.

Arrange on a platter and sprinkle onion on top. Makes about 64 appetizers.

Per appetizer: 10 calories, .4 g protein, .2 g carbohydrates, .8 g total fat, 4 mg cholesterol, 14 mg sodium

CUCUMBER SALAD BOWLS

Preparation time: **About 20 minutes**

Simple and sophisticated accurately describes this appetizer. Smoked salmon, fresh dill, and sour cream are spooned into cucumber cups.

- 2 **medium-size cucumbers (about 1 lb.** *total***), cut into 1-inch-thick slices**
- ¼ **cup (about 2 oz.) chopped smoked salmon or lox**
- 2 **tablespoons sour cream**
- 1 **teaspoon prepared horseradish**
- 1 **tablespoon chopped fresh dill or ½ teaspoon dill weed**
  Dill sprigs (optional)

Using a melon baller, hollow out each cucumber slice, leaving an ¼-inch-thick bowl-shaped shell; reserve scooped-out portions. Drain shells upside down on paper towels.

Meanwhile, chop reserved cucumber; let stand in a colander for several minutes to drain well. In a small bowl, combine chopped cucumber, salmon, sour cream, horseradish, and chopped dill; mix lightly.

Mound salmon mixture into shells. Garnish with dill sprigs, if desired. If made ahead, cover and refrigerate for up to 30 minutes. Makes 10 to 12 appetizers.

Per appetizer: 17 calories, 1 g protein, 1 g carbohydrates, .8 g total fat, 2 mg cholesterol, 43 mg sodium

*For a special occasion, serve Smoked Salmon Mayonnaise
(recipe on facing page) on cucumber rounds. Offer with
Cheddar Cheese Puffs (recipe on page 74), Shrimp &
Feta Fila Triangles (recipe on page 36), and Smoked
Salmon & Herbed Cheese Tarts (recipe on page 36).*

83

STUFFED PASTA SHELLS ITALIANO

Preparation time: About 20 minutes
Cooking time: About 10 minutes

For a Mediterranean touch, add dried tomatoes and Italian parsley to tuna. Then fill oversize pasta shells with the sunny combination for an eat-with-your-fingers treat.

- 12 giant shell-shaped pasta (about 3 oz. *total*), *each* about 2½ inches long
- 2 tablespoons olive oil
- 1 can (6½ oz.) chunk light tuna, drained
- ¼ cup slivered dried tomatoes packed in oil, drained
- 1 tablespoon drained capers
- 1 hard-cooked egg, chopped
- 2 tablespoons mayonnaise
- 1 tablespoon sour cream
- 2 teaspoons Dijon mustard
- 2 tablespoons chopped Italian parsley
  Italian parsley sprigs

In a 5- to 6-quart pan, cook pasta in 3 quarts boiling water just until barely tender to bite (about 10 minutes); or cook according to package directions. Drain. Fill pan with about 2 quarts cold water. Add pasta and oil; when pasta is cool, drain well, shaking gently to remove water.

Combine tuna, dried tomatoes, capers, egg, mayonnaise, sour cream, mustard, and chopped parsley; mix until well blended. Spoon tuna mixture evenly into pasta shells. Arrange on a platter. If made ahead, cover and refrigerate until next day.

Garnish with parsley sprigs. Makes 1 dozen appetizers.

Per appetizer: 106 calories, 6 g protein, 6 g carbohydrates, 6 g total fat, 25 mg cholesterol, 219 mg sodium

---

Pictured on page 70
CHERRY TOMATOES WITH SMOKED OYSTERS

Preparation time: About 10 minutes

With a can of smoked oysters in the cupboard, you can easily make this quick treat. The unusual flavor combination is sure to bring raves from your guests.

- 2 baskets cherry tomatoes
- 1 can (3 oz.) tiny smoked oysters, drained
  Italian parsley sprigs (optional)
  Frisée (optional)

Remove stems from tomatoes. Slice each tomato vertically to within about ¼ inch of base; spread apart and slip in a smoked oyster and, if desired, parsley. Arrange on a platter and garnish with frisée, if desired. Makes about 40 appetizers.

Per appetizer: 4 calories, .3 g protein, .6 g carbohydrates, .1 g total fat, 2 mg cholesterol, 14 mg sodium

---

BELL PEPPER & OYSTER BOATS

Preparation time: About 20 minutes

Almost too pretty to eat: bright bell pepper strips cradle a creamy cheese blend topped with smoked oysters and fresh chives.

- 4 medium-size red bell peppers, stemmed and seeded
- 1 can (3¾ oz.) small smoked oysters, drained
- 2 small packages (3 oz. *each*) cream cheese, at room temperature
- 2 tablespoons lemon juice
- 1 teaspoon celery seeds
- 64 chive pieces (*each* 4 in. long)

Cut each bell pepper lengthwise into 8 equal strips. If necessary, cut larger oysters in half so you have 32 pieces.

Beat cream cheese, lemon juice, and celery seeds until smooth. Spread about 1 teaspoon of the mixture over end of each pepper strip. Top with 1 oyster piece and 2 chives. If made ahead, cover and refrigerate until next day. Makes 32 appetizers.

Per appetizer: 26 calories, .9 g protein, 1 g carbohydrates, 2 g total fat, 9 mg cholesterol, 38 mg sodium

---

CREAMY CRAB IN ENDIVE SPEARS

Preparation time: About 20 minutes

Fresh lime adds refreshing tang to a lightly blended combination of sour cream, cream cheese, and crabmeat.

- 1 small package (3 oz.) cream cheese, at room temperature
- 2 tablespoons sour cream
- 2 teaspoons lime or lemon juice
- ¼ teaspoon grated lime or lemon peel
- 2 tablespoons chopped chives
- ¼ pound crabmeat
  Salt and ground white pepper
  4 to 6 heads Belgian endive, separated into leaves, washed and crisped

Beat cream cheese, sour cream, and lime juice until fluffy. Mix in lime peel, chives, and crab; season to taste with salt and pepper.

Pipe or spoon a dollop of crab mixture into wide part of each endive leaf. Arrange on a platter in a starburst pattern, tips pointing outward. If made ahead, cover and refrigerate for up to 4 hours. Makes about 3½ dozen appetizers.

Per appetizer: 12 calories, .8 g protein, .3 g carbohydrates, .9 g total fat, 5 mg cholesterol, 14 mg sodium

CLAM-STUFFED SHELLS

◆

Preparation time: About 20 minutes
Cooking time: About 10 minutes

A rich blend of horseradish, cream cheese, and clams is tucked into giant pasta shells for a convenient appetizer treat.

You can prepare the shells a day ahead.

32 **giant shell-shaped pasta (about 8 oz. total), each about 2½ inches long**
 1 **tablespoon salad oil**
 2 **large packages (8 oz. each) cream cheese, at room temperature**
 3 **cloves garlic, minced or pressed**
 2 **tablespoons prepared horseradish**
 ¼ **cup chopped parsley**
 4 **cans (6½ oz. each) chopped clams, drained**
    Salt and coarsely ground pepper
    Parsley sprigs

In a 5- to 6-quart pan, cook pasta in 3 quarts boiling water just until barely tender to bite (about 10 minutes); or cook according to package directions. Drain. Fill pan with about 2 quarts cold water. Add pasta and oil; when pasta is cool, drain well, shaking gently to remove water.

Beat cheese, garlic, and horseradish until creamy. Stir in chopped parsley and clams. Season to taste with salt and pepper. Spoon clam mixture evenly into pasta shells. Arrange on a platter and sprinkle with more pepper. If made ahead, cover and refrigerate until next day.

Garnish with parsley sprigs. Makes 32 appetizers.

Per appetizer: 98 calories, 5 g protein,
7 g carbohydrates, 6 g total fat, 24 mg
cholesterol, 57 mg sodium

STEEPED SHRIMP

◆

Preparation time: About 45 minutes
Cooking time: About 3 minutes
Chilling time: At least 1 hour

Let guests enjoy succulent shrimp plain, seasoned in a highly spiced broth, or dipped in a flavored mayonnaise.

 ⅓ **cup vinegar**
 1 **tablespoon each mustard seeds and cumin seeds**
 2 **teaspoons black peppercorns**
 8 **thin quarter-size slices fresh ginger**
10 **cilantro (coriander) sprigs (each about 4 in. long)**
10 **fresh mint sprigs (each about 4 in. long) or 2 tablespoons dry mint leaves**
 2 **tablespoons olive oil**
 2 **pounds medium-size raw shrimp (about 36 per lb.)**
    Mint-Ginger Vinegar (recipe follows)
    Seeded Mayonnaise (recipe follows)

In an 11- to 12-quart pan, combine 5 quarts water, vinegar, mustard seeds, cumin seeds, peppercorns, ginger, cilantro, mint, and oil. Cover and bring to a boil over high heat.

Add shrimp to pan. Cover and remove from heat. Let steep until shrimp are opaque when cut (about 2 minutes). Lift out shrimp and drain. Pour cooking liquid through a fine strainer; reserve seeds but discard liquid, ginger, mint sprigs, and cilantro. Let shrimp cool; then shell and devein. Cover and refrigerate for at least 1 hour or until next day.

Prepare Mint-Ginger Vinegar and Seeded Mayonnaise. Offer with shrimp for dipping. Makes about 6 dozen appetizers.

Per appetizer: 11 calories, 2 g protein,
.1 g carbohydrates, .2 g total fat, 16 mg
cholesterol, 15 mg sodium

Mint-Ginger Vinegar. Mix 1½ cups **rice** or cider **vinegar**, 3 tablespoons **sugar**, and 2 tablespoons

minced **fresh ginger** until sugar is dissolved. Up to 2 hours before serving, add 2 tablespoons minced **cilantro** (coriander) and 2 tablespoons minced **fresh mint** or dry mint **leaves.** Makes about 2 cups.

Per tablespoon: 6 calories, 0 g protein,
2 g carbohydrates, 0 g total fat, 0 mg
cholesterol, .1 mg sodium

Seeded Mayonnaise. Mix 2 cups **mayonnaise,** 3 tablespoons **lemon juice,** and reserved **seeds** from cooking liquid. Makes about 2 cups.

Per tablespoon: 101 calories, .3 g protein,
.7 g carbohydrates, 11 g total fat, 8 mg
cholesterol, 79 mg sodium

GINGERED SHRIMP & CUCUMBER

◆

Preparation time: About 25 minutes
Marinating time: At least 1 hour

Tiny shrimp marinated in rice vinegar and topped with strips of tangy pickled red ginger perch atop cucumber slices in this light, nutritious offering.

 2 **tablespoons rice vinegar**
 1 **teaspoon sugar**
 1 **tablespoon pickled ginger strips**
 ½ **pound tiny cooked shrimp**
 1 **long, slender English cucumber (about 1 lb.), thinly sliced**

Stir together vinegar and sugar until sugar is dissolved. Mix in ginger and shrimp. Cover and refrigerate for at least 1 hour or up to 4 hours.

Arrange 1 or 2 shrimp and a bit of ginger atop each cucumber slice. Makes about 5 dozen appetizers.

Per appetizer: 5 calories, .8 g protein,
.3 g carbohydrates, 0 g total fat, 7 mg
cholesterol, 10 mg sodium

*Present pretty pink packages wrapped with bright green
chives; your guests will appreciate their edible gift,
Shrimp with Tart Dipping Sauce (recipe on facing page).*

Pictured on page 91
PARSLEY SHRIMP BALLS

◆

Preparation time: About 35 minutes
Chilling time: About 2 hours

Tiny shrimp mixed with cheese and celery make attractive, bite-size appetizers that will please a crowd. Reserve some whole shrimp to use as decoration on top.

- 10 ounces small cooked shrimp or 2 cans (5 oz. *each*) shrimp
- 4 ounces Neufchâtel cheese, at room temperature
- 3 tablespoons finely chopped celery
- 1 clove garlic, minced or pressed
- ¼ teaspoon liquid hot pepper seasoning
- 1 teaspoon soy sauce
  About ⅔ cup finely chopped parsley

Rinse and thoroughly drain shrimp; pat dry. Set aside 40 whole shrimp to use for garnish; coarsely chop remainder.

Beat cheese, celery, garlic, hot pepper seasoning, and soy until very smooth. Stir in chopped shrimp just until blended. Cover and refrigerate for about 1 hour or until easy to handle.

Sprinkle parsley on wax paper. For each appetizer, shape 1 teaspoon of the cheese mixture into a ball; then roll each ball in parsley until coated on all sides.

Spear reserved shrimp on wooden picks and stick a shrimp into each ball. Cover and refrigerate for at least 1 hour or until next day. Makes about 40 appetizers.

Per appetizer: 15 calories, 2 g protein, .2 g carbohydrates, .7 g total fat, 16 mg cholesterol, 37 mg sodium

Pictured on facing page
SHRIMP WITH TART DIPPING SAUCE

◆

Preparation time: About 30 minutes
Cooking time: About 4 minutes

Plump pink shrimp neatly tied with bright green chives please the palate as well as the eye. Dip the shrimp in a tangy, shallot-flavored wine vinegar sauce.

- Tart Dipping Sauce (recipe follows)
- 1 pound medium-size raw shrimp (about 36 per lb.), shelled and deveined
  About 36 chives (*each* about 7 in. long)

Prepare Tart Dipping Sauce and set aside.

In a 6- to 8-quart pan, bring 4 cups water to boil over high heat. Add shrimp; reduce heat, cover, and simmer until shrimp are opaque when cut (about 3 minutes). Drain, immerse in cold water, and drain again. Set aside.

In a medium-size frying pan, cook chives in about 1 inch boiling water just until wilted (about 5 seconds); remove immediately with tongs. Tie a chive around center of each shrimp. If made ahead, cover and refrigerate for up to 4 hours.

Arrange shrimp in a dish. Offer with sauce for dipping. Makes about 3 dozen appetizers.

Per appetizer: 11 calories, 2 g protein, .1 g carbohydrates, .2 g total fat, 16 mg cholesterol, 15 mg sodium

Tart Dipping Sauce. Stir together ¼ cup *each* **dry white wine** and **white wine vinegar**, 1 tablespoon *each* minced **shallots** and **chives,** and ½ teaspoon **freshly ground pepper.** Makes about ½ cup.

Per tablespoon: 7 calories, 0 g protein, .5 g carbohydrates, 0 g total fat, 0 mg cholesterol, .5 mg sodium

ASPARAGUS IN BELGIAN ENDIVE

◆

Preparation time: About 20 minutes
Cooking time: About 5 minutes

This elegant, appealing appetizer is easy to prepare. Make it to show off the early spring crop of asparagus while endive is still in season.

If endive isn't available, you can substitute small romaine lettuce leaves.

- 24 asparagus spears
- 24 large outer Belgian endive leaves (about 3 heads *total*) or small inner romaine leaves (about 2 heads *total*), washed and crisped
- ¼ cup olive or salad oil
- 2 tablespoons white wine vinegar
- 2 teaspoons Dijon mustard
  Chopped parsley

Snap off and discard tough ends of asparagus. Peel stalks, if desired. Cut tips to same length as endive leaves; reserve remaining asparagus sections for other uses.

In a wide frying pan, bring 1 inch water to a boil over high heat. Add asparagus; reduce heat, cover, and simmer just until tender when pierced (about 5 minutes). Drain, immerse in ice water, and drain again. Place an asparagus spear in each endive leaf. (At this point, you may cover and refrigerate for up to 6 hours.)

Just before serving, whisk oil, vinegar, and mustard until blended. Pour into a small serving bowl and sprinkle with parsley. Offer with asparagus for dipping. Makes 2 dozen appetizers.

Per appetizer: 24 calories, .5 g protein, .7 g carbohydrates, 2 g total fat, 0 mg cholesterol, 13 mg sodium

Company's coming! You've planned every appetizer down to the last bite. Here are party punches and sparkling spirits, warmed or chilled, to complement your choices. All will welcome guests to your party.

Consider your menu, the time of day, the weather, and, of course, the occasion when you choose your liquid refreshments. For help estimating how much to prepare, see "Great Beginnings" on pages 4–5.

Pictured on page 75
CITRUS SPRITZER

Preparation time: About 15 minutes

Full of spirit, this festive, nonalcoholic drink is a refreshing blend of citrus fruit and sparkling water.

- 4 to 5 large oranges
- 2 to 3 large limes
- 1 bottle (24 oz.) white grape juice
  About 3 cups sparkling mineral water

With a vegetable peeler, cut 3 strips of peel (orange part only), each ½ inch by 3 inches, from 1 orange. Cut 2 strips of peel (green part only), each ½ inch by 3 inches, from 1 lime. Place peel in a pitcher and bruise with a wooden spoon.

Squeeze enough oranges to make 2 cups juice. From 1 lime, cut 5 thin center slices; cut in half and reserve. Squeeze enough of the remaining limes to make ¼ cup juice. Add orange juice, lime juice, and grape juice to pitcher and stir. (At this point, you may cover and refrigerate until next day.)

For each serving, fill glass with ice cubes, juice blend, and water, using about 2 parts juice to 1 part water. Garnish with a lime slice. Makes about 10 servings, ¾ cup each.

Per serving: 74 calories, .4 g protein, 18 g carbohydrates, .1 g total fat, 0 mg cholesterol, 7 mg sodium

PARTY BEVERAGES

◆

BANANA-CITRUS COOLER

Preparation time: About 5 minutes

This frothy, refreshing blend of tropical fruits takes no time to make. For a party with children, prepare it without the rum.

- 2 large ripe bananas, cut into chunks
- ½ cup lime juice
- 1 can (12 oz.) frozen pineapple-orange-banana juice concentrate
- 1 bottle (1 pt. 12 oz.) chilled sparkling mineral water
- 1¼ cups light rum (optional)
- 1 lime, thinly sliced

In a blender or food processor, smoothly purée bananas, lime juice, and concentrate. Pour into a 3-quart pitcher. Add water and, if desired, rum. Stir down foam. Pour into ice-filled glasses and garnish with lime slices. Makes about 12 servings, ¾ cup each.

Per serving: 84 calories, .3 g protein, 22 g carbohydrates, .1 g total fat, 0 mg cholesterol, 5 mg sodium

CRANBERRY-CITRUS COCKTAIL WITH RASPBERRY SWIZZLE

Preparation time: About 20 minutes
Freezing time: About 45 minutes
Cooking time: About 10 minutes

Raspberry swizzle sticks accent this warm, ruby-colored fruit punch, perfect for a holiday party.

- 1 package (12 oz.) frozen unsweetened raspberries, partially thawed
- 1 bottle (64 oz.) cranberry juice cocktail
- 1 *each* medium-size orange and lemon, thinly sliced

Select 24 of the best-looking raspberries. Thread 3 berries on each of 8 thin wooden skewers. Lay skewers on a flat pan and freeze until berries are hard (about 45 minutes); for longer storage, cover and freeze for up to 5 days.

When remaining raspberries are thawed, press through a fine strainer into a 4- to 5-quart pan; discard seeds and pulp. To pan, add juice and orange and lemon slices. Stir over medium heat until steaming (about 10 minutes). Ladle into 8 tall heatproof glasses; add a skewer to each. Makes 8 servings, about 1 cup each.

Per serving: 178 calories, .8 g protein, 47 g carbohydrates, .8 g total fat, 0 mg cholesterol, 6 mg sodium

STRAWBERRY-GUAVA PUNCH WITH SORBET

Preparation time: About 20 minutes
Freezing time: About 1 hour

Fit for any festive occasion, this pink punch showcases strawberry sorbet and fresh strawberries. Offer spoons for the sorbet and fruit.

- 1 quart strawberries, rinsed and drained
- 1 quart strawberry sorbet or sherbet
- 1 can (6 oz.) frozen grapefruit juice concentrate
- 2 bottles (1½ qts. *each*) guava fruit juice drink
- 1 bottle (750 ml.) chilled sparkling wine or 1 bottle (1 pt. 12 oz.) chilled sparkling mineral water

Place half the berries (use the prettiest ones, keeping hulls attached) on a flat pan without touching. Freeze until hard (about 1 hour); for longer storage, package airtight and freeze until next day. Put a 10- by 15-inch pan in freezer. When cold, scoop sorbet into 2-inch balls and place in pan. Freeze for 1 hour; for longer storage, cover airtight and freeze until next day.

Hull remaining berries. In a blender or food processor, smoothly purée berries and grapefruit concentrate. Pour into a 6- to 7-quart punch bowl. Add guava drink and wine; stir well. Add sorbet and frozen berries. Ladle into punch cups or wide-mouthed glasses. Makes about 24 servings, ¾ cup each.

Per serving: 145 calories, .5 g protein, 31 g carbohydrates, .2 g total fat, 0 mg cholesterol, 12 mg sodium

Pictured on page 11
MULLED APPLE-GINGER SPARKLER

Preparation time: About 5 minutes
Cooking time: About 35 minutes
Chilling time: At least 1 hour

Preserved ginger puts an extra punch in cinnamon-flavored apple juice. Just before serving, add sparkling wine or mineral water.

- 2 **cups apple juice**
- ½ **cup chopped preserved ginger in syrup (including syrup)**
- 8 **cinnamon sticks (*each* 2 to 3 in. long)**
- 2 **bottles (750 ml. *each*) chilled brut-style dry sparkling wine or 5 small bottles (10 oz. *each*) chilled sparkling mineral water**

In a 1- to 2-quart pan, boil apple juice, ginger, and cinnamon sticks over high heat, stirring occasionally, until reduced to 1 cup (about 30 minutes); watch closely to prevent scorching. Let cool; then cover and refrigerate for at least 1 hour or until next day. Pour into a small bowl and keep cold.

For each serving, spoon about 2 tablespoons of the apple-ginger syrup into a champagne flute or 6- to 8-ounce glass. Add a cinnamon stick and fill with wine. Makes about 8 servings, ¾ cup each.

Per serving: 161 calories, .3 g protein, 18 g carbohydrates, .1 g total fat, 0 mg cholesterol, 17 mg sodium

BUBBLING MARY

Preparation time: About 10 minutes

Not for the timid, this potent potion should be made with the driest sparkling wine available and fresh lime juice.

- 2 **cups cold tomato juice**
- 1 **teaspoon liquid hot pepper seasoning**
- 2 **tablespoons lime juice**
- 24 **pickled cocktail onions**
- 1 **medium-size lime, cut into 8 wedges**
- 1½ **bottles (750 ml. *each*) chilled brut-style dry sparkling wine or 4 small bottles (10 oz. *each*) chilled sparkling mineral water**

In a pitcher, mix tomato juice, hot pepper seasoning, and lime juice; keep cold. On each of 8 thin wooden skewers, thread 3 onions; place skewers in a tall glass. Put lime wedges in a dish.

For each serving, place an onion swizzle stick in a champagne flute or 8-ounce glass. Pour in ¼ cup of the juice mixture and fill with wine.

Squeeze and drop in a lime wedge and stir with a swizzle. Makes about 8 servings, ¾ cup each.

Per serving: 56 calories, .4 g protein, 3 g carbohydrates, 0 g total fat, 0 mg cholesterol, 152 mg sodium

HOT SPICED PUNCH

Preparation time: About 15 minutes
Chilling time: At least 12 hours
Cooking time: About 5 minutes

Special occasions—and cool nights—call for cups of warming liquid. This spicy drink can be made with grape or cranberry-apple juice.

- 8 **whole cardamom (optional)**
- ½ **teaspoon whole allspice**
- 3 **tablespoons chopped candied ginger**
- 4 **strips lemon peel (yellow part only), ½ inch by 3 inches**
- 1 **cinnamon stick (3 in. long)**
- 2 **bottles (25 oz. *each*) Gamay Beaujolais grape juice or 1 bottle (48 oz.) cranberry-apple juice cocktail**
- ⅓ **cup golden raisins**

Discard cardamom pods, if using. Place seeds in a stainless steel or glass bowl with allspice, ginger, and lemon peel. Slightly crush with a wooden spoon. Add cinnamon stick and juice. Cover and refrigerate for at least 12 hours or up to 2 days.

Pour juice through a strainer into a 2- to 3-quart pan; discard seasonings. Add raisins. Cover and place over medium heat just until hot (about 5 minutes). Serve warm. Makes about 12 servings, ½ cup each.

Per serving: 93 calories, .4 g protein, 23 g carbohydrates, .1 g total fat, 0 mg cholesterol, 6 mg sodium

THAI CARROT SALAD

Preparation time: About 25 minutes

Lettuce leaves hold mini-salads of finely shredded carrots, daikon, and radishes.

- 2 **cups lightly packed finely shredded carrots**
- 1 **cup lightly packed finely shredded daikon**
- ½ **cup lightly packed finely shredded red radishes**
- 2 **tablespoons fish sauce (***nuoc nam* **or** *nam pla***); or soy sauce to taste**
- 2 **tablespoons lime juice**
- ½ **teaspoon sesame oil**
- ¼ **teaspoon sugar**
   Lime slices
   About 16 small butter lettuce leaves (*each* **about 3 in. wide), washed and crisped**

Stir together carrots, daikon, radishes, fish sauce, lime juice, oil, and sugar. If made ahead, cover and refrigerate until next day.

Place vegetables in a small dish; garnish with lime slices. Place lettuce in a basket. Using a slotted spoon, scoop vegetables into lettuce leaves. Makes about 16 appetizers.

Per appetizer: 15 calories, .6 g protein, 2 g carbohydrates, .4 g total fat, 0 mg cholesterol, 7 mg sodium

PICKLED CUCUMBERS

Preparation time: About 10 minutes
Standing time: About 30 minutes
Chilling time: At least 30 minutes

These crunchy cucumbers should disappear in almost as little time as it takes to prepare them—and you can make them with ingredients readily at hand.

- 2 **large cucumbers (about ¾ lb.** *each***), thinly sliced**
- 1 **teaspoon salt**
- ¼ **cup vinegar**
- 1 **teaspoon sugar**

In a large bowl, mix cucumbers and salt; let stand for about 30 minutes. Rinse well and drain. Return to bowl and stir in vinegar and sugar; cover and refrigerate for at least 30 minutes or until next day. Makes 8 servings.

Per serving: 13 calories, .4 g protein, 3 g carbohydrates, .1 g total fat, 0 mg cholesterol, 138 mg sodium

ONION KNOTS WITH PEANUT SAUCE

Preparation time: About 20 minutes
Cooking time: About 5 minutes

Tie blanched green onions into knots ready for dunking in a spicy sauce.

Peanut Sauce (recipe follows)
36 **green onions (including tops)**

Prepare Peanut Sauce; set aside.

Rinse onions and cut off roots. In a 5- to 6-quart pan, cook onions, a few at a time, in 3 quarts boiling water just until green ends are limp (about 20 seconds). Lift out, immerse in ice water, and drain.

Pull off and discard tough outside layers. Tie each onion in a knot so that white end protrudes about 1 inch; trim green end about 1 inch from knot. If made ahead, cover and refrigerate for up to 6 hours.

Offer with sauce for dipping. Makes 3 dozen appetizers.

Per appetizer: 4 calories, .3 g protein, .8 g carbohydrates, 0 g total fat, 0 mg cholesterol, .6 mg sodium

Peanut Sauce. Combine ¼ cup *each* **crunchy peanut butter** and **plum sauce** and 1 tablespoon *each* **lemon juice** and **soy sauce.** Season to taste with **liquid hot pepper seasoning.** Makes about ½ cup.

Per tablespoon: 17 calories, .5 g protein, 2 g carbohydrates, .9 g total fat, 0 mg cholesterol, 38 mg sodium

SESAME LONG BEANS

Preparation time: About 30 minutes
Cooking time: About 13 minutes
Marinating time: At least 1 hour

The flavors of Asia—ginger, sesame oil, rice vinegar, and soy sauce—blend in a light marinade that perfectly suits Chinese long beans. Look for them in Asian markets or well-stocked supermarkets.

- 1 **tablespoon sesame seeds**
- ¾ **pound Chinese long beans, ends trimmed, cut into 6-inch lengths**
- 1 **teaspoon ground ginger**
- 1 **tablespoon sesame oil**
- 2 **tablespoons seasoned rice vinegar; or white wine vinegar mixed with 2 teaspoons sugar**
- 2 **tablespoons soy sauce**
- 3 **tablespoons sliced green onions (including tops)**

In a wide frying pan, toast sesame seeds over medium heat, shaking pan often, until golden (about 3 minutes). Remove from pan and let cool.

In pan, bring ¼ inch water to a boil over high heat. Add beans; reduce heat, cover, and simmer until tender when pierced (about 10 minutes). Drain, immerse immediately in ice water, and drain again.

In a bowl, stir together ginger, oil, vinegar, soy, and onions. Add beans, mixing to coat evenly. Cover and let stand for 1 hour, stirring several times. If made ahead, refrigerate until next day. Just before serving, drain beans. Makes about 40 appetizers.

Per appetizer: 10 calories, .3 g protein, 1 g carbohydrates, .5 g total fat, 0 mg cholesterol, 52 mg sodium

An Asian banquet begins with Marbled Tea Eggs (recipe on page 72), Thai Carrot Salad served in lettuce cups (recipe on facing page), Parsley Shrimp Balls (recipe on page 87), and Onion Knots with Peanut Sauce (recipe on facing page).

ORANGE-FENNEL OLIVES

Preparation time: About 10 minutes
Marinating time: 24 hours

Start with a jar of Greek-style olives and create something special: orange- and fennel-accented olives perfect with an apéritif.

- 1 **jar (10 oz.) Greek-style olives packed in brine**
- 1 **teaspoon fennel seeds**
- 6 **strips orange peel (orange part only),** *each* **½ inch by 2 inches**
- 1 **tablespoon sherry vinegar or red wine vinegar**

Drain olives, reserving brine. Return half the olives to jar; add fennel seeds, orange peel, remaining olives, vinegar, and reserved brine. If liquid doesn't cover olives, add enough water to cover. Replace lid and let stand at room temperature for 24 hours, shaking occasionally. If made ahead, refrigerate for up to a month.

Drain olives, reserving orange peel, and place in a bowl with peel. Makes 8 servings.

Per serving: 121 calories, .8 g protein, 3 g carbohydrates, 13 g total fat, 0 mg cholesterol, 1,165 mg sodium

---

Pictured on page 75
SNAP PEA KNOTS

Preparation time: About 30 minutes
Cooking time: About 30 seconds

Quickly cooked snap peas retain their color and crunch. String cheese ties add a festive touch.

- ½ **pound sugar snap peas**
- 2 **to 3 oz. string cheese**

Snap off or trim ends of peas, pulling strings away from both sides. In a wide frying pan, cook peas in 1 inch boiling water until bright green (about 30 seconds). Drain, immerse in ice water, and drain again. (At this point, you may cover and refrigerate until next day.)

Separate cheese into strings slender enough to tie easily. Loosely tie a string of cheese around center of each pea. Makes about 4 dozen appetizers.

Per appetizer: 7 calories, .5 g protein, .7 g carbohydrates, .1 g total fat, .8 mg cholesterol, 11 mg sodium

---

MINTED PEAS & ALMONDS

Preparation time: About 15 minutes
Baking time: About 8 minutes

Guests can scoop this salad into lettuce leaves and enjoy the tasty mixture of peas, celery, and green onions in a minty yogurt dressing.

- 1 **cup slivered almonds**
- ⅓ **cup mayonnaise**
- ¼ **cup plain yogurt or sour cream**
- 1 **teaspoon Dijon mustard**
- 1 **tablespoon chopped fresh mint leaves or 1 teaspoon dry mint leaves**
- ¼ **teaspoon salt**
  Dash of ground red pepper (cayenne)
- 1 **package (10 oz.) frozen tiny peas, thawed**
- 2 **stalks celery, finely chopped**
- ¼ **cup sliced green onions (including tops)**
  About 24 butter lettuce leaves, washed and crisped

Spread almonds in a shallow pan. Bake in a 350° oven until golden (about 8 minutes). Set aside.

Stir together mayonnaise, yogurt, mustard, mint, salt, and pepper until blended. Add peas, celery, onions, and almonds; mix lightly. If made ahead, cover and refrigerate until next day.

Offer with lettuce leaves for scooping. Makes about 2 dozen appetizers.

Per appetizer: 66 calories, 2 g protein, 3 g carbohydrates, 5 g total fat, 2 mg cholesterol, 67 mg sodium

---

FRUITED TABBOULEH

Preparation time: About 1¼ hours
Cooking time: About 8 minutes
Chilling time: At least 1 hour

Dried apricots and dates give this crunchy cracked-wheat salad a whole new dimension. Wrap in a lettuce leaf for salad on-the-go.

- 1 **cup** *each* **bulgur and cold water**
- ¼ **cup slivered almonds**
- ⅓ **cup** *each* **chopped pitted dates and slivered dried apricots**
- ½ **teaspoon ground cinnamon**
- 2 **tablespoons chopped fresh mint leaves or 1 tablespoon dry mint leaves**
- 2 **tablespoons salad oil**
- 1 **tablespoon** *each* **lemon juice and honey**
  About 24 red leaf lettuce leaves, washed and crisped

Rinse bulgur several times. Combine with water and let stand for 1 hour. Drain any liquid that is not absorbed. Meanwhile, spread almonds in a shallow pan. Bake in a 350° oven until golden (about 8 minutes). Let cool.

Mix bulgur with almonds, dates, apricots, cinnamon, mint, and oil. Blend lemon juice and honey; stir into bulgur mixture. Cover and refrigerate for at least 1 hour or up to 3 days.

Offer with lettuce leaves for scooping. Makes about 2 dozen appetizers.

Per appetizer: 60 calories, 1 g protein, 10 g carbohydrates, 2 g total fat, 0 mg cholesterol, 2 mg sodium